FIXING
BROKEN BRITAIN

First published in 2023 by
Alun Drake Books
9 rue des Petits Pres
67300 Schiltigheim
France

Paperback ISBN 9791041519057

Cover design and typeset in Adobe Caslon Pro and Trade Gothic by Namkwan Cho

ALUN DRAKE

FIXING BROKEN BRITAIN

A BLUEPRINT FOR NATIONAL REVIVAL

AD BOOKS

CONTENTS

INTRODUCTION

Let me tell you a story...

Once upon a time there was an island lying off the coast of north-west Europe. Because of its sea moat, the place was last invaded by a King called William and his friends, who were all called Norman. But that was a very long time ago. From this island sailed forth men of action, who founded the biggest empire the world has ever seen, and clever men on the island invented machines which gave it industrial power before any other nation. When war came to Europe and later to the world, the island nation was always on the winning side. But after the last great conflict, it was exhausted from so much fighting, and lost nearly all its great empire.

Then it was humiliated in Egypt by the American States that were United; one of its former colonies that had recently become a 'superpower.' But not long after the Egyptian bust up, the Americans became the island's closest friend, with a relationship that everyone said was very special, and they even let the islanders share their secret weapon, which was so powerful it could destroy the whole world. This made the islanders feel better for a while, but they were still annoyed at being constantly labelled 'the sick man of Europe.' So, the island tried to join a club of neighbouring countries that were not sick, but their request was rudely rejected several times by the leader of the Gauls.

When he lost power, they politely asked again if they could join, and this time the response was positive. But although nobody ever called them 'the sick man of Europe' again, some of the islanders kept discussing whether it was worth staying in the club. They said they would never be happy until they were free of any attachments to their neighbours. Eventually, it was decided to resolve the matter by holding a vote on whether to remain in the association. A tiny majority voted to leave, which deeply saddened the large minority who wanted to stay—and also the other club members, who had grown used to the islanders' strange ways. So, the island nation said goodbye to the continental organisation, and headed for the uplands that were rumoured to be exceedingly sunny. And they all lived happily ever after.

We all like a good fairy tale, but from time to time it is necessary to touch base with reality. And the reality is that however glorious Britain's past may have been, its future is looking decidedly bleak. An article in *The Financial Times* predicted that, by 2024, the average British household would be poorer than its Slovenian equivalent—and, by 2030, it would also be overtaken by the average Polish family.[1] The prime suspect for this downward trajectory is the country's exceptionalism: its seemingly unshakeable belief that it can, and indeed should, do things its own way, without reference to other countries. It is often expressed overtly in assertions—often made by politicians but widely shared by the public—that it is either already 'the greatest country in the world,' capable of 'world beating' feats of initiative and originality, or that this supreme status lies just around the corner. The underlying assumption, never voiced explicitly, is that British people, and in particular the English, are innately superior to the citizens of all other nations. Nowhere is this better expressed than in the assertion attributed to Cecil Rhodes: 'Remember that you are an Englishman and have consequently won first prize in the lottery of life.'[2]

Not all manifestations of this British exceptionalism are harmful. Often, they are simply quirky in an *Alice in Wonderland* kind of way, where nothing is quite what it seems. Take the name of the country, for example. Not only are we 'Great Britain', but we are also 'The United Kingdom' (a distinction that I suspect is lost on most people living outside of Northern Ireland). This creates problems when checking in for flights. In the drop-down menu for registering your nationality, do we look for 'British,' 'Great Britain' or 'United Kingdom?' It's so much simpler if you come from France or Brazil.

Then there's the British Museum, which reminds me of the Monty Python cheese shop which didn't sell any cheese. With so little of British origin within its impressive walls, it should probably be renamed 'The Museum of Exhibits From Countries We Used To Rule,' or simply 'The British Empire Museum.'

The UK's central bank is known as the 'Bank of England' but also regulates the money supply and fixes interest rates for Wales, Scotland and Northern Ireland.

Why do Brits who emigrate to other countries insist on calling themselves ex-pats (short for 'expatriate'), while describing Polish people living in the UK as immigrants? If it's to signal that they intend to return permanently to the UK one day, then this also applies to many people living temporarily in Britain. So, either we start referring to British people living on the Costa del Sol as immigrants, or we should describe the Polish residents of Manchester as ex-pats. Some would say the real reason for the double standard is that for British people living abroad, the word 'immigrant' has a negative connotation, so they prefer to be known as 'ex-pats,' which conjures up images of pith-helmeted, white-suited administrators of the Raj sipping a gin and tonic on the veranda while watching a game of cricket.

And speaking of sport, how come every other country that belongs to the United Nations can field only one national football team, but we have four (England, Wales, Scotland and Northern Ireland)? Or that a Welsh bowler can play for the England cricket team and a scrum-half from Northern Ireland can pull on a Jersey for Ireland's rugby XV? Why, at the Olympics, is it team GB and not team UK, given that there are athletes from Northern Ireland in the British delegation? (They can also choose to compete under the auspices of the Olympic Federation of Ireland.)

Such anomalies may be faintly amusing but they have no great bearing on the nation's future prospects. Other contradictions, however, are more insidious and betray a worrying mixture of apathy and muddled thinking.

For example, our nuclear deterrent is invariably described as 'independent' but—since we bought the Trident missiles from the Americans, who also play a major role in their maintenance and modernisation—it can clearly be nothing of the kind. The French, who developed and built everything themselves, have an independent deterrent. We do not.

According to our Police, Crime, Sentencing and Courts Act, you can be sent to prison for four years for rape and other serious sexual assaults and 10 years for defacing a statue, apparently in recognition of the latter's 'emotional, symbolic value.' In a similar example of topsy-turvy legal priorities, victims of violent crime are awarded £2,400 in compensation if their injury requires an eye operation.

Damage to your reputation is valued much more highly: a good libel lawyer can win you an award of up to £300,000, thanks to Britain's peculiarly generous defamation laws.

Identity cards are a feature of everyday life in most European countries. For many, they substitute for a passport when travelling around the EU. But many politicians in the UK have a visceral aversion to them, arguing that Britain is not a 'papers, please' or a 'Big Brother' society. Yet, while the idea of the state keeping track of its citizens with a piece of plastic not dissimilar to a driving licence is anathema to such libertarians, few seem to bat an eyelid at the UK having more CCTV and speed cameras per head than any other European country, or that British consumers readily share their personal data with a wide range of private companies, from social media platforms to online retailers, banks, and supermarkets.

For a country that purports to put a supremely high value on national sovereignty, it is indeed curious that we have casually sold off more than half our home-grown companies to foreigners. Chemicals giant ICI was a household name until it was sold to the Dutch conglomerate AkzoNobel in 2008. Soon, the new owners were closing factories in the UK, with thousands of job losses, and profiting from the scientific and industrial expertise the British firm had built up over many decades. Department store Debenhams was bought by three American private-equity firms, who proceeded to asset strip their new acquisition before loading it with debt and selling it on for a profit, leaving it severely weakened.

Other foreign transfers of iconic British brands include Rolls Royce and the Mini (to Germany), Jaguar and Land Rover (to India), Corus (formerly British Steel, to India), chocolate maker Cadbury (to the USA) and supermarket chain Asda (also to the USA). When the high street chemist chain Boots was sold to an Italian company in 2007, it had to move its headquarters from Nottingham, where it had been based for 161 years, to Zug in Switzerland. Before the takeover, Boots paid £89m in tax in its final year as a British-registered company. Soon, it was paying the lion's share of its tax liability to the Swiss exchequer, with a tiny percentage going into UK Treasury coffers.

More recently, in 2021, Britain's largest semiconductor producer, Newport Wafer Fab (formerly Inmos), was sold to Nexperia, a Dutch subsidiary of China's Wingtech Technology. Even more controversially, the UK's most successful tech company, ARM, based in Cambridge's so-called Silicon Fen, was sold in 2016 to Japanese tech investor SoftBank. ARM's software is embedded in leading smartphone brands, including the iPhone, and it also plays a key role in enabling everything from fitness trackers to server farms. Allowing the sale of ARM to a foreign buyer is regarded by many industry insiders as one of the government's two biggest strategic industrial blunders of the past decade (the other was the sale of artificial intelligence start-up Deepmind to Google in 2014).

As Oscar Wilde's overbearing creation, Lady Bracknell, might have put it: 'To lose one national champion may be regarded as a misfortune. To lose more than 50 per cent of them looks like carelessness.' In contrast, on the other side of the Channel, enlightened patriotism trumps corporate greed. When US drinks giant PepsiCo tried to bid for French yoghurt maker Danone, President Chirac declared it was a national strategic asset, and therefore could not be sold to a foreign firm. In similarly patriotic fashion, Spain beat off an attempt by German energy group E.ON to take over Madrid-based Endesa. The truth is that in the UK, when it comes to selling off iconic national assets, money talks and sovereignty walks.

How can a country, that makes such a big show of caring for its past, care so little about investing in its future? We are truly world-beating at militarised pageantry, whether it's organising royal coronations, weddings and funerals, changing the guard at Buckingham Palace, or trooping the colour. Two of our coveted national awards for civic contribution, the OBE and the CBE, pay homage to our former empire. With more than 5m members, the National Trust does an incredible job of conserving Britain's natural, historical and architectural heritage. The nation's meticulously curated past is hugely popular with the public. So how can the same country be so slapdash and lackadaisical when it comes to securing its future status?

Nothing is more essential to our daily survival than water. Yet we waste this precious resource on a colossal scale, with 25 per cent of it leaking through decaying Victorian pipes. The water companies are fixing the leaks at a snail's pace—replacing just 0.05 per cent of the 200,000-mile network every year, compared with a European average replacement rate that is ten times as fast. Even more shockingly, since 1990, the UK population has grown by 10m to 67m—an 18 per cent increase—yet not a single new reservoir has been built. With drought and unprecedentedly high temperatures becoming an ever more frequent fixture of British summers, this lack of investment will be felt more keenly with each passing year. The UK's infrastructure chief, Sir John Armitt, has described the government's approach to water security as 'keeping (its) fingers crossed.'[3]

There's a slightly different story with gas. Britain used to have ample storage capacity, but, in 2017, the Rough facility in the North Sea was closed in order to save £75m a year in maintenance costs. That decision left the UK with enough gas in reserve for just five winter days of normal consumption, or two per cent of annual demand. The Netherlands, a country four times smaller than the UK, has a gas storage capacity nine times as big, while Germany has 16 times and Italy 18 times more storage than the UK. To put the gas situation into the water context, it's as if we've been filling in reservoirs instead of building new ones.

In the National Health Service (NHS), a similar long-term policy, of putting cost-cutting before capacity-building, led to the system's near collapse in recent years. International studies show that the UK has half as many hospital beds per head of population as France, and a third as many as Germany. The discrepancy is even greater for intensive care beds. Moreover, we have a much higher bed occupancy rate than either of our two largest European neighbours. It all smacks of a 'just in time,' 'penny-pinching' and 'seat of the pants' approach to essential public services—which leaves them ill prepared for any shock to the system.

In 2012, London hosted the Olympics, which opened with an inspiring ceremony celebrating Britain's contribution to the world, including the industrial revolution, some of the world's best loved popular music and the Internet. As we will see in later chapters, there were some curious omissions, and it was strange to see the NHS feature so prominently, given its obvious shortcomings, but, on the whole, the event reflected a confident country, optimistic about its future. Little more than 10 years later, despair has replaced optimism. Admittedly, Covid and the war in Ukraine have contributed significantly to the downturn, but the chaos that followed the Brexit vote was entirely self-inflicted. The chronic under-performance of essential services like energy, water and railways are the result of wrong-headed decisions made by successive governments over many decades. Writing in the *New Statesman*, Martin Fletcher summed up the dire state of the nation:

'Today, we are a country that has lost its way—divided, dispirited, dysfunctional and shorn of common purpose. We are a diminished Britain, regarded with a mixture of pity, bewilderment and scorn by much of the rest of the world. We are a broken Britain whose economy and public services are perilously close to collapse. By almost any measure—living standards, economic growth, physical and mental health, life expectancy, environmental cleanliness, homelessness, happiness—we are considerably worse off now than a decade ago.'[4]

We can blame individual politicians for this miserable state of affairs, but the real culprits are our dysfunctional political institutions and our apartheid-style education system. Take our so-called democracy. We have an unelected head of state, an unelected upper house, a lower house elected by an unfair voting system, a political culture that scorns compromise, consensus and cooperation, a ramshackle uncodified constitution and the most centralised state in Europe. Unaccountable press barons, often not even resident in the UK, exercise undue influence over politicians of all shades of opinion. It would have been a miracle if such a shoddy set up had resulted in successful long-term policy making. Our current predicament has been entirely predictable. Even the best political operators in the world would have struggled to obtain optimal outcomes from an out-of-date, sub-optimal system. But our politicians are far from world beating. A century-old aircraft might still be able to take off safely if it is maintained by excellent engineers and flown by outstanding pilots. Without such skilled personnel, it is just a matter of time before such an old plane crashes.

As for our education system, its shortcomings are exposed by the UK being the only country in Europe where school fees far outstrip the costs of attending university. Some private schools charge up to £50,000 a year per child—nearly five times their university equivalent. And remember that there are many more years spent at school than in higher education, even taking further degrees like masters and PhDs into account. Lambrook prep school in Berkshire hit the headlines in August 2022 when it was announced that the Duke and Duchess of Cambridge (now the Prince and Princess of Wales) would be sending their children there. Full-time nursery care for a three-year-old at Lambrook costs more than £13,000. That's 40 per cent more than you would pay for studying physics at an Oxford college (currently £9,250 per year). Teaching a seven-year-old at the same establishment would set you back nearly £20,000 a year, which is 50 per cent more than studying for a master's in advanced computer science, also at Oxford.

While many working-class families struggle to pay for their children to go to university, middle and upper-class parents must breathe a sigh of relief when their offspring become undergraduates, given that higher education is so much cheaper than private schooling. This disparity indicates that private schools have far greater resources than their state counterparts, in everything from superior teacher/pupil ratios to state-of-the-art facilities. The flip side is that far too many state school pupils do not receive the education they deserve (and the country needs), which in turn means that the UK's stock of human capital is of poorer quality than it would otherwise have been, had resources been more fairly allocated. This puts us at a considerable disadvantage when competing against countries with more equitable education systems.

The huge mess in which the UK currently finds itself reminds me of the Humpty Dumpty nursery rhyme—who can put broken Britain back together again? The answer is that a massive systems upgrade is needed. Politicians will always claim that constitutional and electoral reform is a distraction from more pressing day-to-day matters, but the reality is that we will never succeed in tackling the latter if we keep shirking the former. If we fail to address the fundamental issues raised in this book, we will never catch up with the more modern democracies that are our main competitors. We will instead be overtaken by the likes of

Poland and Slovenia. If we persist with our current malfunctioning system—putting social class, tradition and privilege before fairness and efficiency—we will be like a sprinter trying to compete in a race with a ball and chain attached to their ankle. We would never dream of handing down the same ancient car or computer from one generation to the next, so why should this be the right approach for our political system? The choice we have is between passionately campaigning for a modern British democracy or sticking with our present arrangements and continuing to decline.

The rest of this book is devoted to exposing the extent of the problem—and suggesting some realistic solutions. Humpty Dumpty never did get put back together again, despite the best efforts of all the King's horses and all the King's men. I therefore prefer another classic children's story, which at least had the positive outcome of speaking truth to power and calling out—literally—the metaphorical elephant in the room. Please think of the author as the innocent child in the story of the emperor's new clothes. I just hope you won't be shocked by the naked truth.

CHAPTER 1

ANYWHERE BUT WESTMINSTER

Why our parliament is in the wrong place

You can tell a great deal about a country's political system by how it refers to its parliament. In Germany, it's simply the *Bundestag*. In France, it's nothing more and nothing less than the *Assemblée Nationale*. Most countries refer to their parliaments by their names. But, as in so many other areas, the UK does things differently. We constantly refer to Westminster, the London borough where our parliament happens to be located. No other European democracy does this (though the US Congress is often referred to as 'Capitol Hill'). It's as if we can't imagine our parliament being based anywhere else than London SW1. While other democracies think nothing of moving their parliaments either within the same city (as Australia did in Canberra) or from one city to another (from Bonn to Berlin in Germany's case), the UK seems intent on keeping its national parliament on the same site in perpetuity. It's impossible to imagine BBC's Radio Four's Sunday evening politics show changing its name from *The Westminster Hour* to *The Mile End Hour* or *The Solihull Hour*, if the parliament were to move to East London or the West Midlands respectively.

Nevertheless, throughout the centuries there have been several opportunities to decamp from Westminster. Perhaps the best opportunity came in 1834 when the building burned down. King William IV offered Buckingham Palace as an alternative law-making venue (he is said to have intensely disliked the monarch's main London residence). But MPs politely turned down his proposal and rejected similar plans to relocate to Charing Cross or St James's Park. Instead, the leading architect, Sir Charles Barry, was commissioned to re-build the parliament in the Gothic Revival style (although some maintain that another architect, Augustus Pugin, should take much of the credit, especially for the interior features and for the Big Ben clock tower). The result was one of the world's most iconic buildings, which has been a UNESCO World Heritage site since 1987. It has attracted the attention of countless artists, most famously the French impressionist Claude Monet, who painted a series of views of the building in different weather conditions. But, as we shall see, inspiring architecture does not necessarily make for inspired political decision making. As a venue for a modern parliament, the Palace of Westminster would never win any prizes.

The next chance to do a runner from SW1 came in May 1941, when Luftwaffe incendiary bombs hit the Commons chamber and the roof of Westminster Hall. The fire service calculated it was impossible to save both, so they concentrated their efforts on protecting the Hall. As a result of that decision, the Commons chamber was destroyed by the fire, which spread to the members' lobby, causing the ceiling to collapse. All that was left of the chamber was a smoking shell. It was the perfect excuse to permanently move parliament to another London location, but instead it was decided to re-build it in the original, rectangular, style. Churchill maintained that this form was responsible for the two-party system—which, for him, was the essence of British parliamentary democracy. 'We shape our buildings and afterwards our buildings shape us', he observed.[1]

So, what's wrong with the Palace of Westminster? The clue lies in the building's elitist name, which encapsulates its priggish nature. The palace was modelled along the lines of a Pall Mall gentlemen's club, as an exclusive establishment aimed at keeping the public out—and the privileged members of its two chambers protected and pampered, behind its imposing walls. The exterior of the building is meant to intimidate, while the sumptuous interior is designed to impress. But, from a professional politician's point of view, there's nothing impressive about the House of Commons. For a start, its green leather benches can seat only 427 elected representatives. The other 223 have to remain upright during important debates, making ours the most upstanding, if not necessarily outstanding, parliament in the world. More seriously, can you imagine a company boardroom with fewer chairs than the number of directors, or a classroom with fewer desks than pupils?

But even for those MPs lucky enough to be able to park their posteriors, the seating lacks one of the most basic tools of any modern democracy. Among the G20 countries, we are the only one whose national parliament is not equipped with electronic voting. In every other venue, not only does each MP have his or her designated seat, but they also have a button to enable electronic voting in situ. By contrast, Westminster's arbitrary first come, first seated arrangements preclude the installation of individual voting buttons. To cast their votes, MPs have to physically walk through the 'for' and 'against' lobbies, where they are manually counted. This laborious procedure can take up to 20 minutes per vote, and obviously discriminates against MPs with mobility issues.

But the worst aspect of the House of Commons chamber is undoubtedly its rectangular form. The opposing benches' design means that the government and the opposition line up like two clashing armies, ready to go into battle. Appropriately, MPs facing each other across the chamber are separated by a minimum distance of two sword lengths. Indeed, each MP still has the right to bring a sword into the building, provided they hang it in a special cloakroom before entering the chamber. If an MP wishes to defect from the government to the opposition or vice versa, they must demonstrate their commitment to switching sides by physically walking across the floor of the House, in plain view of their colleagues.

The official parliament website puts a positive spin on this deliberately confrontational design, which, it claims, 'helps to keep debates lively and robust but also intimate.' I'm not sure whether heckling or shouting down your opponent counts as 'intimate.' Perhaps 'intimidating' would be a better description of the type of loutish behaviour that would never be tolerated in more civilised parliaments, including the assemblies in Belfast, Cardiff and Edinburgh. Bizarrely, although MPs are allowed to shout abuse across the chamber and join in with weird displays of mass groaning, there is a strict ban on clapping, which is seen as disrespectful to the traditions of the house, although the rule is sometimes ignored by more emotional members.

In contrast to the uncouth din of the Commons debating chamber, it is whispers that are the problem in the rest of the building, according to political commentator Ian Dunt. Speaking on the *Oh God What Now?* podcast, he attributed what has often been labelled as the Westminster psychodrama to the nooks and crannies nature of the building: 'It's sort of designed for hysteria really because it's based on conversations in corners and murmurs and plots. The tea rooms, the little rooms here and there ... There are never any rooms, outside of arguably the select committee rooms, that are designed for people to meet and cooperate. It's designed as a place of corners, for the whipping around of rumour and innuendo.'[2]

It's also a place where subsidised alcohol is easily obtainable, thanks to the palace's numerous bars. In 2021, more than £200,000 was spent on drinks, despite the bars having been closed for half of the year thanks to Covid. Like clapping, smoking is banned in the Commons chamber, so boxes of snuff (powdered tobacco) are provided free of charge for MPs to snort before entering the room. According to a *Sunday Times* investigation in 2021, there is evidence that snorting a different kind of substance may be rife elsewhere in the building. Traces of cocaine were found in 11 out of 12 toilets tested for the drug.

So how does the UK parliament compare to its foreign equivalents? Two architects at XML, an Amsterdam-based consultancy, made a study of the parliaments of all 193 United Nations member states. Max Cohen de Lara and David Mulder van der Vegt wrote the definitive reference book, entitled simply *Parliament*.[3] In it, they explain that there are only five types of parliamentary layout. Westminster is home to the original 'opposing benches' design, which reflects the political system that evolved in England after the Magna Carta placed limits on royal power for the first time in 1215. Based on the chapel where it first met, the Commons chamber is composed of long rows of benches, which were occupied originally by the clergy on one side and nobles on the other, with the King in the middle. When this motley crew were replaced by MPs, the nave became the parliamentary lobby and the choir stalls the benches, with the Speaker sitting where the altar had been. This form has been copied mainly by countries from the former British Empire, including Canada, Zimbabwe and Jamaica (however, in contrast to Westminster, the seating arrangements in most of these chambers correspond with the number of MPs).

In Europe, only the Czech Republic has adopted the UK model. Most other continental countries chose the fan-shaped 'semicircle' or 'hemicycle' layout that blurs political dividing lines and encourages cross-party cooperation. Two of the other three models ('horseshoe' and 'circle') are variations on the same circular theme, but the fifth type of layout, known as 'classroom,' is typically found only in authoritarian countries, where parliamentarians are expected to bow to authority rather than challenge or monitor it. Hence the parliaments of China, North Korea, Myanmar and Russia consist of rows of desks facing towards the podium, ensuring that attention is focused on the bigwigs sitting there.

Professor Matthew Flinders, from Sheffield University, specialises in the political impact of parliamentary design.

He says purpose-built modern parliaments—that are much more open, light, spacious and transparent—encourage a more professional way of working: 'What you have encapsulated in the Westminster model is an amateurish approach to politics, with the basic assumption that politicians are doing a normal job during the day and politics is just a sideline, almost a hobby sport. If you look at the way the new parliaments are designed, it's very much with a professional working environment in mind. However, just because you have space, light and windows doesn't mean the politics conducted within the building might not be secretive or elitist. However, I still think that the structure and architecture of a building itself symbolises a certain approach or set of expectations around how we do politics.'[4]

One young newly elected Labour MP, Laura Pidcock, was so shocked by the palace's unwelcoming architecture and the arcane practices of its denizens, that she dedicated a significant portion of her maiden speech to listing its shortcomings: 'Turning to this place, this building is intimidating. It reeks of the establishment and of power; its systems are confusing—some may say archaic—and it was built at a time when my class and my sex would have been denied a place within it—because we were deemed unworthy. I believe that the intimidating nature of this place is not accidental. The clothes, the language, and the obsession with hierarchies, control and domination are symbolic of the system at large.'[5]

But, if you think the upper level of the palace is dysfunctional, wait until you venture downstairs into the basement below central lobby, known affectionately by the long-suffering team of maintenance staff as 'the cathedral of horrors.' It looks like a museum of Victorian technology, but sadly it is what passes for state of the art in this venerable building. A Heath Robinson-like contraption of cylinders and pumps is all that stands between parliament and a tsunami of sewage. Installed in 1888, these steam-powered sewage ejectors pump human waste and rainwater into the main London drain. But ancient plumbing is only one of a wide range of hazards threatening the safety of the palace. There are constant fire dangers, with modern electrical cables crammed next to asbestos-covered steam pipes. In the event of a blaze, a byzantine system of vents could allow smoke and flames to spread rapidly throughout the building.

Since 2016, there have been at least 25 fires in the building, most of them admittedly minor, but an indication, nevertheless, that Westminster could easily succumb to the same fate as the *Notre Dame* cathedral in Paris. Asbestos is another risk. The toxic substance is found in no fewer than 2,500 places on the parliamentary estate. A leak from a Victorian steam pipe could send asbestos hurtling through the ventilation system, posing a severe health risk to the building's 6,000 passholders, among them cooks, clerks, cleaners, contractors, journalists, police officers, and, of course, MPs and peers.

Indeed, in an incident in 2021, 117 people were accidentally exposed to asbestos. They will now have to undergo regular health checks for the next 40 years. Other risks of working at Westminster include falling masonry, as the outside of the building crumbles (in 2018 a football-sized lump dropped 70 metres from a stone angel on the Victoria Tower, luckily landing in a garden) and flooding (water cascading from a leaking roof into the Commons chamber during a debate on Brexit in 2019 forced the sitting to be suspended). The annual cost of maintaining and repairing the palace has been soaring in recent years, from £30m in 2007 to nearly £130m in 2018. In 2021, a strategic review concluded that 'The 150-year-old building is falling apart faster than it can be fixed.'[6]

As BBC reporter Chris Bowlby put it, in a radio documentary exposing Westminster's dangerously decrepit technical infrastructure: 'The building that's meant to represent the British constitution is a kind of national monument to make do and mend, with lots of bits from different eras bolted on to each other and much left unwritten—like where all these cables and vents end up, and what they actually do.'[7]

Insiders have known about parliament's dirty little secret for years. A joint committee of MPs and peers published a report in 2016 which warned that the palace 'faces an impending crisis which we cannot responsibly ignore ... there is a substantial and growing risk of either a single, catastrophic event, such as a major fire, or a succession of incremental failures in essential systems.'[8]

The response to this apocalyptic warning has been a proposal to move both the Commons and the Lords out of the place for up to eight years, to allow an extensive programme of modernisation, known as 'restoration and renewal.' The cost of repairs for this option was initially put at £4bn—the equivalent of the budget for building Heathrow Airport's giant Terminal Five. But a more recent study, carried out by an independent 'sponsor board,' estimated the cost at between seven and £13bn, with MPs and Lords moving out for between 12 and 20 years. These gargantuan sums shocked parliamentarians to such an extent that they decided to abolish the group which produced them. So, then, it's back to the in-house drawing board to come up with a more reasonable bill for the taxpayer and shorter absences for the politicians. Said one MP: 'How can we tell the public that, during a cost-of-living crisis, we are planning to spend nearly as much money as it cost to build London's Elizabethan line (better known as Crossrail) on renovating just one building?'

An alternative plan is to shut down parts of the palace over a much longer period, to carry out a rolling programme of upgrading work that would allow the building to continue hosting parliamentary proceedings. The problem with this solution is that the flagging electricity, drainage and heating systems are all unitary and should ideally be replaced in one go. A staggered sequence of works would drastically increase the costs and pose security risks for MPs, who would have to walk along the pavement in front of the palace to access the chamber from their offices. It's estimated that the incremental approach could take up to 30 years to complete.

For a fraction of the cost of any of the renovation options, a new parliament could be built in East London, where land is relatively plentiful and cheap, compared with central London. Moving to another part of the country would be still less expensive, but many argue that proximity to Whitehall is important, especially for those MPs with ministerial responsibilities. We don't have to look far for inspiration. The Senedd, or Welsh Assembly, located in Cardiff Bay, was the brainchild of Lord (Richard) Rogers. He described how the chamber was deliberately sunk beneath the public space, a configuration which according to him 'deliberately reflects how politics should operate … Transparency, for passers-by and visitors, and for the people watching the democratic debates below, is the driving force.'[9] His acclaimed design cost £41m to build, just one per cent of the lowest estimate for restoring the Palace of Westminster.

The Scottish Assembly follows the same principles of transparency, light and public access (politicians use the same entrance as everyone else) but it was a much more controversial project. Designed by the Catalan architect Enric Miralles, who died during the building's construction, it suffered from huge cost over-runs, believed to have been caused by multiple modifications. From an initial estimate of £40m, the cost of construction soared tenfold to £414m. Mind you, even that inflated sum represents a mere 10 per cent of the least expensive proposal for renovating the Palace of Westminster.

If our elected representatives don't want to move to a (comparatively) cheap and striking new building but prefer to spend vastly larger sums of taxpayers' money on renovation, then perhaps they should consider the example of the *Reichstag* in Berlin. Built by Bismarck, burnt down by Nazis, and stormed by the Red Army, this was the building chosen to house the *Bundestag*, Germany's federal parliament, following the historic decision to move all government and parliamentary institutions from Bonn, the sleepy Rhineland capital of West Germany, to brash and booming Berlin, the reunified country's new capital and largest city. The prestigious project was awarded to another leading British architect, Sir Norman Foster. His design saw the building completely gutted, although anti-Nazi graffiti left by victorious Soviet soldiers in 1945, such as *'Hitler kaput'* was carefully preserved.

Foster's signature innovation in the £250m project was the construction of a huge transparent glass and steel dome, open to the public via a spiral walkway. Today, it's the building's most popular feature, making the *Reichstag* the second most visited attraction in Germany. From the dome, natural light descends to the debating chamber far below. Visitors at the top of the structure can symbolically look down on their representatives, reminding the politicians that they are beholden to the people who elected them. A similar approach in Westminster could replace the opposing benches design with the popular 'hemicycle' (circular) shape, with individual desks for MPs, equipped with computers and electronic voting buttons (for nostalgia's sake, their chairs could be made of green leather, recycled from the original Commons benches). But, as things currently stand, the two parliaments are vastly different.

As John Kampfner explains in his book, *Why the Germans Do it Better: Notes from a Grown-Up Country*, buildings help to define behaviour and parliamentary environments define a nation's reputation. In the case of Germany, 'Reunification was taken as an opportunity to improve the country, with a new political architecture striving for stability and transparency … Like most modern parliaments, the (German) parliamentary chamber is arranged in a hemicycle. It is designed for consensus, not confrontation. Reputations are made in committees and constituency work, rather than by rhetorical flourishes.'[10] In contrast, Kampfner is damning in his criticism of a ramshackle British parliament, steeped in eccentricity: 'With its absurd quirks, its flunkies in ridiculous outfits, it removes parliamentarians from the lived experience of voters and elevates tradition over pragmatism. Sadly, it is more synonymous with the pantomime leering and jeering of set-piece interactions in the chamber, rather than the earnest and more collaborative work that most MPs would like to be associated with.'[11]

If cost is the key factor, then the new build solution wins—hands down. Equally, if money is no object, then we may as well follow Germany's example and imaginatively re-configure the Palace of Westminster, forsaking the unambitious current plan to restore it on a like-for-like basis. Either way—new building or new-look building—we would send an optimistic message about Global Britain's new role and status. So why is there no discussion of either of these bolder alternatives? Professor Flinders thinks one reason is that MPs expended excessive amounts of energy on Brexit. But he also detects a more cynical factor at play: 'The real reason why the politicians don't want to leave is that the two main political parties realise that the physical structure locks in a two-party system that works in their favour. If they were to move to a different design model their power base and the way the structure supported them would obviously be undermined. So, there is a very strong attempt going on at the moment by the two main parties to thwart any redesign because they know it would work against them.'[12]

Frustrated by the lack of progress, many people who

favour moving to a new building now believe their best hope is a catastrophic failure of the Palace's ancient infrastructure. Professor Flinders explains the rationale for this subversive desire for a benign technical breakdown: 'What is actually needed at Westminster to force the issue and to facilitate a serious and balanced discussion about the relationship between architecture, design and politics would be for there to be a crisis. A lot of people within the Palace of Westminster were very open. They used to call it the Guy Fawkes option. They thought that the only way that the issue would ever get taken seriously would be if there was some sort of major flood, catastrophe, a sewage explosion, a fire, the asbestos is found to be leaking all over the place—something like that, which would really create a window of opportunity. I am not saying that it's a good thing to happen, but the alternative is what we have at the moment, which is a slow, laborious, muddling through system which may well deliver something that is hardly better, if anything, than what we have at the moment.'

But in the event of a Guy Fawkes induced decision to move our parliament to another location, what would become of the Palace of Westminster? Wouldn't we be faced with two huge bills—one to build a new parliament and another to restore the old one? One way to minimise the cost would be to turn this prime piece of central London real estate into a money-spinning *Museum of Democracy*, complete with souvenir shops (*Black Rod Bling* or *Amazing Mace*), restaurants (*Order, hors d'oeuvre!* or *Brasserie Bercow*, named after a controversial speaker of the House of Commons) with a luxury themed hotel (*The Big Ben* or *The London Lobby*) and bookshops (*White Paper* for adults, *First Reading* for children).

Meanwhile, the Commons chamber could finally realise its true destiny as a theatrical venue, with actors in period costume, re-enacting debates featuring such legendary sparring partners as Gladstone and Disraeli, Lloyd George and Churchill, as well as more contemporary matchups like Heath and Wilson, Thatcher and Kinnock, Blair and Hague, Johnson and Starmer, etc. After all, if foreign tourists are prepared to pay handsome sums to gawk at wax dummies at *Madame Tussauds*, they will surely be willing to fork out a similar small fortune for the privilege of entering a fabled *Harry Potter-esque* structure to experience at first hand such searing parliamentary put-downs as Denis Healey comparing Geoffrey Howe to a dead sheep and Vince Cable's depiction of Prime Minister Gordon Brown's rapid transformation from Stalin into Mr Bean. Money raised from tourism would, within a decade or two, easily recoup the cost of modernising the building and adapting it to its new role, nourishing public nostalgia for a bygone age of Punch and Judy politics.

Sceptics can draw inspiration from Down Under, where

Old Parliament House in Canberra is now the *Museum of Australian Democracy*. The cut and thrust of contemporary Aussie politics takes place at nearby New Parliament House, which, as the name suggests, is a professionally designed parliament equipped with all mod cons, such as enough chairs and desks to go around, and sewage systems that don't threaten to explode. Hooks for hanging your sword, however, are notable by their absence.

Children's author Philip Pullman has his own Guy Fawkes option, which he explained in a tweet: '1. Move everyone out of the Houses of Parliament. Clear every building within half a mile. 2. Blow the place up. 3. Rebuild it in a way that works and doesn't fawn over a vulgar idea of the past. Much of our diseased politics is embodied in that building.' I have to agree with his last sentence. Given the immense cost of renovating Westminster and the acute dangers to life and limb it poses for the thousands who work there, it should be a no-brainer that the best solution is to move to a bold new building, preferably outside London, fit for democratic purpose and symbolic of a confident, modern nation fully committed to upgrading its way of doing politics.

Clinging to tradition for the sake of retaining arcane ceremonies and practices—involving Black Rods, woolsacks, snuff boxes and swords—speaks volumes about a lack of commitment to progress and a fear of change. A country whose parliamentarians are so irrationally and emotionally attached to their ancient surroundings that they are incapable of modernising them is not likely to successfully navigate the shocks and challenges of the 21st century.

CHAPTER 2

HOUSE OF (MARKED) CARDS

Replacing the Lords with a lottery

On 9 November 1953, the celebrated Welsh poet, Dylan Thomas, died after drinking 18 straight whiskeys at one of his favourite New York watering holes. The coroner's report described it as 'a massive insult to the brain.' More than 30 years later, the then Prince Charles ridiculed an architect's proposal to extend the façade of London's National Gallery as 'a monstrous carbuncle on the face of a much loved and elegant friend.' Our upper parliamentary chamber, the House of Lords, merits a fusion of both descriptions: it is at once a massive insult to democracy and a monstrous carbuncle on the face of British public life.

To understand why, let's start by doing some number crunching. If there were Olympic medals for the size of an upper house, the UK would easily qualify for the silver. At more than 800-strong the House of Lords is beaten to the gold only by the National People's Congress of China, which has nearly 3,000 delegates (at 650 the House of Commons gets the bronze medal, so the UK comes in at second and third in the global rankings by size of legislature. If the competition was limited to democracies, the UK's bloated parliament would take both gold and silver). By way of contrast, the United States Senate consists of a mere 100 members, even though America's population is five times bigger than the UK's. Which means that, if the UK had the same size population as the USA, we would have a world beating House of Lords of nearly 4,200 members (thereby depriving the Chinese of their gold medal).

Or looked at another way, if we downsized to match the US ratio of senators to population, our upper house would have just twenty lords (and if we made the same calculation for the House of Commons, it would shrink to about 80 MPs, thereby solving the perennial seating capacity problem on the green benches). Based on North American population comparisons, the House of Lords is currently about 40 times too big. Moreover, it's also highly unusual to have an upper chamber bigger than the lower one. The only other countries that fall into this top-heavy category are China, Kazakhstan and Burkina Faso, none of them liberal democracies.

But even if you adopt a relaxed, size-doesn't-matter, attitude, the House of Lords is still way out of line with leaner and meaner upper chambers when it comes to value for money. For example, unlike US senators, a Lord doesn't have to do a stroke of work to earn his or her £313 daily signing-in allowance. That's because for many (some would say most) peers, being a member of the House of Lords is a privilege rather than a job. Many of their lordships have taken full advantage of the generous daily payment (topped up by travel allowances for those living outside London). A *Sunday Times* investigation in February 2020 found that the cost of expenses and allowances claimed by peers in the year to March 2019 soared by 29 per cent to an annual pay-out of £23m (and this sum does not include the chamber's yearly running costs, which amount to an additional £100m). The paper reported that the average tax-free payment was £30,827, with one Labour peer claiming £80,000, having signed in at Westminster for 159 out of a possible 161 days. In return for this sum, he spoke 17 times in the chamber and was not a member of any committee. Around 100 peers claimed a total of more than £1m, without having made any spoken or written contribution to the House during the relevant period.[1]

The system is wide open to abuse, as even a former Lords Speaker admitted in an interview for the BBC documentary series *Meet the Lords* in 2017. Baroness D'Souza described how, on leaving late one evening, she noticed a peer getting out of a taxi, having instructed the cabbie to keep the engine running while he went into the Lords. He emerged ten minutes later, got into the taxi and left. The anecdote's clear implication was that the peer was on the fiddle, having signed on for his daily allowance before doing a runner. She told the BBC: 'There is a core of peers who work incredibly hard, who do that work, and there are, sad to say, many, many, many peers who contribute absolutely nothing but who claim the full allowance.'[2] Unsurprisingly perhaps, the *Daily Mail's* headline for their article on this story was 'House of Frauds.'[3]

The average Lord—if there is such a thing—is hardly representative of the country as a whole. White, male and stale would be a good catch-all description. Only six per cent are from ethnic minorities. Three out of four are men. One in two are more than 70 years old, and there are only 29 who are under 50. Incredibly, only two out of the 834 are under 39. Former Conservative prime minister Lord Stockton, better known as Harold Macmillan, joked that: 'If, like me, you are over 90, frail, on two sticks, half deaf and half blind, you stick out like a sore thumb in most places, but not in the House of Lords. Besides, they seem to have a bar and a loo within 30 yards in any direction.'[4]

In the BBC documentary mentioned above, Lord Tyler, who represented the Liberal Democrats on constitutional affairs, called it: 'The best day care centre for the elderly in London. Families can drop him or her off and be sure that the staff will look after them, with nice meals subsidised by the taxpayer, and they can have a snooze in the afternoon in the chamber or in the library.'[5]

And 92 places in the Lords are reserved for the so-called 'blue bloods,' or hereditary peers, descendants of the same noble families who used to dominate the chamber before the Blair government's 1999 reform that abolished the vast majority of them. When one of the remaining 92 dies, a tiny clique of aristocrats elects a replacement. So, it's technically wrong to claim that peers of the realm are unelected. It's just that to qualify for a vote in this bizarre by-election you have to not only be an aristocrat, but a male one, thanks to the centuries-old tradition of passing the noble title to the first-born son (the custom known as 'male primogeniture.')

This situation explains why only one of the 92 hereditary lords is female. However, five daughters of peers have challenged this blatant sex discrimination by taking their case to the European Court of Human Rights in Strasbourg, arguing that, because they cannot inherit their father's titles, they are barred from taking seats in the Lords, and that this breaches two articles of the European Convention on Human Rights, one concerning gender discrimination and the other—wait for it—the right to a free and fair election.

These aristo-men-only by-elections even have manifestos, which are shorter than many tweets, thanks to a maximum 75-word limit. The record for brevity is held by Lord Plender, who wrote just one word—'Duty'—to describe his motivation for applying. Lord Geddes ran him close with 'Brains; breadth; brevity'. The appropriately named Seventh Earl of Limerick's manifesto took the form of a poem with a morbid punchline:

> 'The Upper House knows none so queer
> A creature as the Seatless Peer
> Flamingo-like, he stands all day
> With no support to hold his sway
> And waits with covert eagerness
> For 92 to be one less.'[6]

But not all hereditary peers are lusting after a seat in the House of Lords. When the Labour politician, Anthony Wedgwood Benn, inherited his father's title and became Viscount Stansgate, he had to resign his seat as an MP, because peers are barred from standing for election to the Commons. In 1963, he won the right to renounce his title and thereby became eligible again for a seat in parliament's lower house. Tony Benn ridiculed the concept of hereditary legislators with his usual dry sense of humour: 'If I went to the dentist and as he began drilling my teeth he said, "I'm not a dentist myself, but my father was a very good dentist," I think I would jump out of his chair!'[7] Although one of Tony Benn's sons, Stephen, has since reclaimed his birth-right to an aristocratic title, his father was surely on the right track in highlighting the absurdity of allowing aristocrats to play a leading role in a modern democracy. The only other countries to do this are Tonga and the Kingdom of Lesotho.

Almost as odd as the quota for 92 noble lords is the allocation for Bishops and Archbishops from the Church of England, where 26 seats in the upper chamber are reserved for the 'Lords Spiritual.' This tradition dates from medieval times, when society was divided into three estates: the clergy, the nobility and everybody else. The Archbishops of Canterbury and York, and the Bishops of London, Durham and Winchester, all automatically get a seat. The other 21 are normally the longest-serving bishops, though this rule has been suspended in order to allow women who become bishops to automatically enter the Lords, regardless of seniority, in an attempt to move towards gender balance after centuries of male domination. Currently there are 21 men and five women.

The Lords Spiritual are supposed to represent the views and interests of all faiths, not just their own, but it is hard to imagine them simultaneously seeing the world from the standpoint of Catholics, non-conformist Protestants, Muslims, Jews, Hindus, Sikhs, Rastafarians, Humanists and all the other faiths that make up modern-day Britain. Remember, too, that the religious contingent is exclusively English, with no religious leaders from Wales, Scotland or Northern Ireland. By adding geographical insult to ecclesiastical injury, the UK thus belongs to a highly exclusive club of countries—the Vatican and the People's Republic of Iran are the only other members—that allow clerics to make laws that apply to all citizens, regardless of their religious beliefs. By contrast, our nearest neighbours of comparable size—France, Germany and Italy—go to great lengths to keep politics and organised religion separate from one another.

Apart from aristocrats and bishops, who are the other lords and how do they get there? Since 1999, when the Blair government's Parliament Act abolished all but 92 of the aristocrats, but retained the bishops, the vast majority of Lords are chosen by the prime minister of the day. These are the so-called 'life peers,' appointed for the rest of their lives but unable to pass on the title to their descendants. Most of the names he or she puts forward for formal royal approval are members of his or her political tribe, but other party leaders, except for the SNP and Sinn Fein, who both boycott the Lords (Sinn Fein also boycotts the Commons) can nominate candidates for inclusion in the PM's list.

Former MPs make up the bulk of the names, rewarded either for their length of service or, according to some cynics, so that someone younger can stand in the safe Commons seat that they are obliged to vacate in order to move to the Lords. Of the non-politicians, distinguished civil servants, diplomats and other high-ranking professionals are well represented. There is also a sprinkling of celebrities from the worlds of sport, arts and media. Past examples include cricketers Ian Botham and Rachel Heyhoe-Flint, broadcasters Melvyn Bragg and Joan Bakewell, *East Enders* star Michael Cashman, architects Richard Rogers and Norman Foster, and crime novelist Ruth Rendell.

There is another route to a life on the red benches, which leads exclusively through the House of Lords Appointments Commission. These are the so-called 'People's Peers,' selected for their expertise on specialist subjects, or outstanding records of public service. This was another Tony Blair initiative. The initial idea was to get upstanding citizens such as doctors and nurses into the Lords rather than party apparatchiks and superannuated ministers. Without exception, they would become so-called crossbenchers, without any party-political allegiances.

But, when the first batch of People's Peers was named in 2001, there was widespread disappointment at the absence of ordinary members of the public. Among the 11 men and four women selected in the first open contest for membership of the Lords, which attracted 3,000 applicants, there were seven knights, the wife of a peer, three professors and two others who had already been honoured. They included an ex-Commissioner of the Metropolitan Police, a former Chief Executive of the BP oil company and a career diplomat who was the UK's permanent representative to the European Union and the United Nations. All but four were mentioned in *Who's Who?*, the Bible of the British establishment.

Lord Stevenson, who chaired the Appointments Commission, observed that: 'You haven't got your hairdresser in this list, but if you go back to our criteria, one of them is that the human being will be comfortable operating in the House of Lords.' This remark drew a sharp rebuke from John Edmonds, then leader of the GMB union, whose members include hairdressers: 'This club remains as exclusive as ever. If the House of Lords is going to slam its doors so arrogantly in the face of working people, then the time has come to tear the door off its hinges and bulldoze the building to the ground.'[8] (Presumably his union also includes bulldozer drivers).

Charter 88, the constitutional pressure group, dismissed the appointments as a gimmick to distract attention from root-and-branch reform of the Lords. Indeed, time seems to have vindicated their cynical verdict. In 2020, there were only about 60 'People's Peers' out of 834, and their number is growing at a snail's pace—on average, no more than two new appointments per year, with none at all made in 2016.

When it comes to prime ministerial appointments, critics have two main lines of attack. The first is that there are simply too many Lords already, so new members effectively thwart efforts to reduce the size of the chamber. The second is that, of those appointed, a suspiciously high number have made generous donations to party funds. Occasionally, the ennoblements are suspect for other reasons. In December 2020, Boris Johnson disregarded security service advice and appointed Evgeny Lebedev, the co-owner of *The Evening Standard* and the *Independent*, as Lord Lebedev of Hampton and Siberia. Lebedev's father is a former Russian spy who was based in London during the late 1980s and early 90s.[9]

Harold Macmillan was the first prime minister with the power of appointment. In 1958, his government brought in the Life Peerages Act, which, for the first time, allowed the creation of peerages lasting only for a lifetime, in contrast to those passed down the generations as a birthright. It is said that after his notorious cull of cabinet members, which tabloid newspapers dubbed 'the night of the long knives,' he compensated many of his victims with seats in the House of Lords.

But it was only after the abolition of all but 92 of the hereditary peers in 1999 that prime ministers could appoint their replacements on a much larger scale. Tony Blair took first prize for creating the most—374 over a decade—but David Cameron created them fastest, with 245 during his six years in power. Theresa May was the first prime minister to promise to slow down the rate of increase, and she kept her word: a mere 43 new peers were appointed during her three-year tenure at Number 10. But Boris Johnson nominated 36 additional Lords, drawing the ire of Lord (Norman) Fowler, the Speaker of the upper chamber at that time, who said in July 2020:

'This list of new peers marks a lost opportunity to reduce numbers in the House of Lords. The result will be that the House will soon be nearly 830 strong—almost 200 greater than the House of Commons. That is a massive policy U-turn. It was only two years ago that the then prime minister, Theresa May, pledged herself to a policy of "restraint" in the number of new appointments. This followed a report by a special lord speaker's committee proposing that numbers be reduced to 600. This was debated by the Lords itself, commanding overwhelming support. The big opportunity was for the current government to take forward the movement for reform. I emphasise that this is not a question of personalities. It is a question of numbers and the abandonment of an established policy to reduce the size of the house.'[10]

One of Boris Johnson's picks was billionaire businessman Michael Spencer, who is also a leading donor to the Conservative Party, having given them £6m through his private investment group, IPGL. He is among 22 former donors to the main parties who were awarded peerages in the last 13 years, according to a special report by *The Financial Times*.[11] Between them, they contributed £50.4m, either personally or through related companies, with the bulk of the money going to the Tory party. And 15 of the 22 donors are Conservatives, four are Liberal Democrats and three are Labour supporters. The biggest gifts include £3.5m from Stanley Fink, £8.2m from Anthony (JCB) Bamford and £8.6m from Michael Farmer, all of them to the Conservative Party.

Angus MacNeil, the Scottish Nationalist Party MP who instigated a police inquiry into the cash-for-honours affair in 2006, described the *FT*'s analysis as: 'The stuff of banana republics.' He said it was time for the UK to take lessons from other countries: 'Proper democracies don't have people who donate a cool million magically finding themselves in parliament.' But Professor Meg Russell, the director of University College London's Constitution Unit, is less troubled by the donation aspect of prime ministerial appointments. She is more concerned that the House of Lords Appointments Commission (HOLAC), which selects the People's Peers, plays only a very limited role in judging the suitability of party-political nominees. She told the *Financial Times* that in her view, 'Parties should really have to state what qualifications their nominees have to sit in the Lords, and nominees should be interviewed by HOLAC before being appointed.'

The one thing everyone can agree on is that the House of Lords needs to be either reformed or replaced, described by insiders as the 'mend it or end it approach,' because the current situation is so obviously unsustainable. But, to understand the different proposals for change, it is first necessary to consider the specific role that the upper chamber plays in British democracy.

The most valuable, and time consuming, work of the Lords is to scrutinise, revise and amend government legislation that may have been hastily drafted by the House of Commons, often because of time pressures. With their more flexible timetable, the Lords can go through draft laws with a fine-tooth comb, proposing amendments to be considered when the bill returns to the Commons. Specialist expertise is often brought to bear in debates and committees, which take place in a polite atmosphere, more collegiate and less partisan than the Commons.

The Lords can also delay government bills by up to one year, with the aim of giving ministers and other involved parties time to consider the full implications of proposed new laws. But one thing the Lords will never do, in line with a practice known as the 'Salisbury Convention,' is to vote against a government bill in its final stages if that bill was part of the ruling party's election manifesto. This is a nod in the direction of the superior democratic legitimacy of the elected House of Commons, compared with the unelected House of Lords.

Reform of the Lords has continued on and off for more than a century. It started with Lloyd George, who was so frustrated at having what he called his 'People's Budget' blocked by the Lords that he described the aristocratic peers as '500 men chosen at random from the ranks of the unemployed.'[12] The showdown ended with the upper house losing its veto over government bills.

After the Second World War, their delaying power was limited to one year by Attlee's Labour administration, and, in 1999, came Tony Blair's mass expulsion of all but 92 of the hereditary peers, in what was meant to be the prelude to a fully elected upper chamber. But, like an abandoned building site, work on reforming the House of Lords ground to a halt in the years that followed, with multiple efforts to restart the process ending in failure, usually in the form of a defeat of reform proposals in the House of Commons.

Historian Peter Hennessy, himself a life peer, has described Lords reform as the Bermuda Triangle of British politics, after the mysterious zone in the north-west Atlantic where many planes and ships are said to have vanished without trace.[13] Parliamentary time has been occupied with Brexit and Covid, so there are currently no reform initiatives. Nonetheless, there exist several oven-ready proposals on the kitchen table, waiting for political chefs to warm up. They fall into two categories: on the one hand, the baby steps approach of incremental change, and, on the other, the big bang alternative of executing a bold, far-reaching solution. Within these categories, there are only four options: a fully appointed chamber, a fully elected chamber, a mixture of appointed and elected or something completely different.

Professor Russell is an incrementalist. For her, the top priority is to reduce the number of peers to between 550 and 650. To achieve this target, she recommends introducing a compulsory retirement age, encouraging early retirement and calling on prime ministers to exercise restraint in the creation of new peers. She also favours ending the aristocratic by-elections and expelling members convicted of serious criminal offences: at present, they can take 'leave of absence' and return to the chamber after being released from prison or whenever the scandal they were involved in has been forgotten.[14]

In his book *Renovation: Rebuilding UK Politics,* journalist Roger Parry advocates a more radical solution. He estimates it might take up to a decade to put into practice. In terms of numbers, he wants to go further than Professor Russell, and reduce the upper house to no more than 400 members, selected in four different ways. He says 100 would be people's peers, chosen by the House of Lords Appointments Commission, in a continuation of today's system. Another 100 so-called expert peers would be drawn from a wide range of fields including academia, health, accountancy, architecture and the law.

The third category, of regional/national peers, would be the largest cohort: 150 of them would be drawn from the UK's nine regions and three nations. The idea would be for each region or nation to vote for around a dozen peers, once every five years. Unlike MPs, they would not be representatives and would have no constituency duties. They would, however, be expected to ensure that regional and national concerns are reflected in debates. The remaining 50 members of the upper house would be nominated by the prime minister, as happens today, but on a much larger scale. The result, argues Parry, would be a chamber that would have 'a much higher level of multidisciplinary expertise, a strong set of regional roots and still provide an outlet for senior ministers and others to be kicked upstairs: an ideal group to scrutinise draft legislation and to hold MPs to account.'[15]

Labour has promised to abolish the House of Lords if it wins the next general election. The party wants a democratically elected Assembly of the Nations and Regions.[16] The new chamber would have a wider remit than the House of Lords: as well as revising legislation, it would also monitor standards in public life and protect the constitution, including the current distribution of power between London and the capitals of the other home nations. Labour's plan does not specify how members of the new assembly would be elected but does recommend that upper-house elections should not coincide with those of the Commons.

Fleet Street commentators appear to agree that the House of Lords does indeed need urgent reform. The *Observer* columnist Andrew Rawnsley describes the upper house as 'a gilded mockery of Britain's claim to be a fully developed democracy' and 'a kind of private members' club that pays you for attending.'[17] As long as it lacks democratic legitimacy, he believes, 'the Lords can never be more than a constitutional speed bump for the executive to roll over.'

The most likely reform being discussed behind the scenes is a second chamber composed of directly or indirectly elected members of the Scottish, Welsh and Northern Ireland parliaments, and the mayors and other leaders of England's largest regional authorities. The aim would be to create a less London-centric upper house that could give a voice to the whole country, perhaps thereby reducing the prospects for an independent Scotland. It has been suggested the new chamber could be re-located to York, to underline its non-Metropolitan credentials.

The problem with this plan, and indeed with all recent reform proposals, is that most MPs do not want the Lords to acquire more democratic legitimacy and the enhanced authority and power that would inevitably come with it. In the words of Andrew Rawnsley: 'A ridiculous second chamber persists because many MPs think it is in their interest to keep the Lords ridiculous.'[18]

That's why my preferred reform proposal is one that would not make MPs feel threatened. It is an outlandish idea, quite literally, because its origins lie far from British shores, in the Athens of Ancient Greece. But despite the concept's foreign provenance, its basic principle has been in operation in our country for hundreds of years. The Greek name is 'sortition,' or selection by the drawing of lots. In Britain, we use it for jury service, asking randomly selected members of the public to sit in judgement on their peers.

In this new version of an ancient practice, the House of Lords would consist of randomly selected members of the public—let's call them 'Peers in Parliament.' They would be drawn from the UK regions, in proportion to the size of their population, and with a 50/50 gender balance. Their numbers and length of service is up for discussion. One solution would be for them to serve for a year, with the same salary as MPs. As with jury service, their employers would be compensated during their absence. We would need perhaps 400 of them. A small number of the most active and experienced members of the current House of Lords could be retained as mentors and advisers for the new arrivals, explaining parliamentary procedures and chairing working groups, committees and debates.

Given the necessary training and advice, there is no reason why the system could not work. If ordinary citizens can serve effectively as jurors in complicated fraud trials, why could they not cope with scrutinising parliamentary legislation? All the evidence from studying citizens' juries and deliberative assemblies in the UK and elsewhere suggests that they can do the job, provided their role is one of scrutiny and their responsibilities are clearly defined.

The Irish Republic is the Rolls Royce role model for citizens' assemblies, having laid the groundwork for referendums on two of the most sensitive issues for this staunchly Catholic country: gay marriage and abortion. Evidence suggests that the assemblies' recommendations—for legalisation in both cases—strongly influenced many voters to back the changes, which won convincing majority support at the polls, and are now enshrined in law.

In the German-speaking part of Belgium, they have taken things even further by placing randomly chosen members of the public in the regional parliament, alongside elected MPs, making it the first permanent citizens' assembly in the world. The concept is called the *Eupen* model, after the region's capital city.

In their book, *The Athenian Option*, dedicated to explaining how democratic jury service would work, Anthony Barnett and Peter Carty make clear that a sortition-based House of Scrutiny would support, not supplant, the House of Commons, by providing the lower-house legislators with input from a truly representative cross-section of the British public.[19] It is true that the House of Lords already provides high-quality feedback on draft laws, but it lacks credibility and legitimacy as an institution, for all the reasons outlined above. Having the same work done by peers in parliament would be a significant democratic upgrade on the current set-up.

For starters, it would immediately nullify all the jibes and accusations of privilege, partisanship and cronyism aimed at the aristocrats, bishops, political retirees and party donors who pack Westminster's second chamber. A reformed upper house composed entirely of peers in parliament would also greatly benefit from an injection of youth, gender balance, ethnic diversity, geographical spread and a genuine social mix of classes, trades and professions.

In another pro-sortition book, *People Power*, author Richard Askwith argues that a reformed second chamber would have an electrifying effect on our democracy: 'Not because the people's peers were any wiser than the peers we have now, but because, in contrast to our current peers, they visibly represented the people. In democracy, legitimacy is everything.'[20]

As well as being more authentically representative than their predecessors, the new occupants of the red benches would also be free of party-political allegiances, and therefore better placed to provide independent and dispassionate scrutiny and oversight of the legislative process. The parliaments in Westminster, Cardiff, Belfast and Edinburgh, as well as metropolitan mayors in Birmingham, Manchester, Liverpool and elsewhere, illustrate that we already have enough elected representatives, without adding another ermine-clad layer in the Lords. To misquote Michael Gove, it is not experts, but professional politicians, that we have had enough of.

And there's another upside to banning party politics from the second chamber. To date, the Scottish Nationalist Party (SNP) and the Irish republican party, Sinn Fein, have consistently shunned the Lords. Sortition would be a way of by-passing their boycott, allowing randomly selected SNP and Sinn Fein voters a voice in upper house deliberations for the first time—another significant step forward for democracy.

When Lloyd George made his famous quip about the House of Lords consisting of '500 men drawn at random from the ranks of the unemployed,' the Liberal prime minister nicknamed the Welsh Wizard came close to hitting the constitutional nail on the political head.

What broken Britain badly needs is a quick fix for the upper house, based on a radical re-write of the Lloyd George dictum. Putting 400 men and women, drawn from the ranks of the electorate, into the second parliamentary chamber would be a great formula for turbo-charging British democracy.

CHAPTER 3

CAN WE HAVE THAT IN WRITING?

It's time to codify our constitution

What do the UK, Israel and New Zealand have in common? Answer: none of them has a codified constitution. In Britain's case, most experts agree on the main reasons for this omission. One is that our country never had what one writer called a 'constitutional moment.' These historical turning points usually happen during times of extreme national distress, disruption or liberation. They most often coincide with revolution (France in 1789), defeat in war (Germany in 1945) or gaining independence from a colonial master (America in 1776 or India in 1947). We have not been successfully invaded for nearly 1,000 years, have always been on the winning side in European wars and have not been colonised since Roman times, and so missed out on such moments of national introspection.

The other reason for not formalising our constitution is

the well-worn mantra: 'If it ain't broke, don't fix it.' According to this school of thought, our informal and ingeniously flexible constitution has served us well over the centuries, helping us to overcome a series of challenges, including the industrial revolution, two world wars and the loss of empire. To attempt to put everything down on one piece of paper would be to open too many complicated and controversial Pandora's boxes, with the attendant risk of inflaming public opinion on multiple fronts, or so the argument goes.

But what exactly has been working so well for all this time? Very few people, even among the political class, can give a coherent explanation of our constitution. Jonathan Lis, of the British Influence think-tank, describes it as 'this charming period-drama constitution of old school ties and gentlemen's conventions.'[1] The Institute for Government's Hannah White is equally whimsical in her depiction of the British constitution as: 'An unusual beast: a centuries-old amalgam of precedent, convention and rules scattered across numerous texts, laws and institutions, unlike any other in the world in its longevity and lack of codification.'[2]

For P.G Wodehouse's foppish Bertie Wooster, just saying the words 'the British constitution' required such an effort that he used it as a tongue twister to determine his state of sobriety. Even Queen Elizabeth II once confessed in public that, 'The British constitution has always been puzzling and always will be.'[3] The late law lord Tom Bingham put it rather more negatively: 'Constitutionally speaking, we now find ourselves in a trackless desert without map or compass.'[4] But, despite this lack of orientation, most Britons are familiar with the building blocks of our democratic system.

To begin with, there's the executive, or machinery of government, which decides and puts into practice national policy. In the UK, it consists of the prime minister, the cabinet and junior ministers, supported by the civil service. The government/executive is the big beast of the democratic jungle, controlling the lion's share of the levers of power, when it has a working parliamentary majority.

The legislature, or parliament, scrutinises laws before voting on them, and approves the taxes that pay for government policies. But, in reality, hard-pressed backbench MPs often find it difficult to balance their time-consuming constituency work with the arguably much more important oversight role of holding the executive to account. And, for politicians harbouring ambitions of gaining high office, objective scrutiny might in any case take a back seat to blind government loyalty.

The third major component is the judiciary. These are the law courts and judges responsible for interpreting and upholding the law of the land, regardless of political considerations. However, it's only since 2011 that the UK's highest court has been fully independent from the world of politics. Before that, the country's top judges were the so-called law lords, who sat in the upper house. But, for the past decade, that role has fallen to the Supreme Court, which, despite being located only a short walk from the Palace of Westminster, no longer counts among its number any legally qualified peers of the realm.

Last, but certainly not least, there's the head of state, in our case the King, whose largely symbolic role includes appointing the prime minister and giving the final seal of approval to new laws once they've passed through parliament. In most other democracies, the head of state is an elected president, who serves a fixed term of office.

Constitutions are like instruction manuals for cars, televisions and kitchen appliances: you normally refer to them only when you have an issue with the device or when it has stopped working altogether. In other words, an effective constitution is designed to solve problems. When everything is going well you shouldn't need to consult it at all. A good constitution, like an effective instruction book, should be both comprehensive and comprehensible, explaining in clear terms what to do in a wide range of situations, including conflicts and disputes. Its primary function should be to define how the system's three main centres of power (executive, legislature and judiciary) relate to each other, including the extent of each one's authority, and how these relations can be changed if need be.

Secondly, a constitution lays out the rights of citizens.

These include basic rights such as the right to a fair trial, to free speech and to privacy. It should also clearly define the circumstances in which the state can legitimately breach our fundamental rights, for example by spying on us, or sending us to prison. Lord Bingham believed that codified constitutions which set out a few clear principles were vital to allow 'any citizen to ascertain the cardinal rules regulating the government of the state of which he or she is a member.' In addition, he thought they also help to 'inculcate a constitutional awareness which is particularly important in the increasingly polyglot, multicultural, religiously diverse, plural society which this country has become.'

A constitution normally also defines how many levels of government a country has and explains their relationship. In the case of a federal system like those of the USA or Germany, it's particularly important to distinguish the responsibilities of the national government from those of the states.

Finally, all constitutions express their country's aspirations. These might be life, liberty and the pursuit of happiness (the USA), to be liberal and not fascist (Germany); to be Islamic (Iran) or to be non-racist (South Africa). An example closer to home was cited by historian and author Linda Colley, while explaining in a *Financial Times* article why countries with codified constitutions rarely abandon them: 'This is because written constitutions frequently do more than simply set out on paper specific legal and political provisions. They supply a way of shaping and proclaiming a country's desired brand. Just think how Ireland has been able to use recent constitutional amendments in support of abortion and same-sex marriage to proclaim and advertise its modernity and its liberation from previously strict Catholic tutelage.'[5]

In countries with codified constitutions, these provisions are enshrined in special statutes which enjoy a higher status than other laws of the land. Constitutional laws cannot be changed by a simple majority in parliament. They are said to be 'entrenched', or protected, and can normally only be amended or repealed by a so-called 'super majority', which usually means a two-thirds majority of both houses of the legislature. In some democracies, this is notoriously difficult to achieve. For example, in the USA all efforts to tighten gun control regulations by challenging the Second Amendment's 'right to bear arms' have failed, thanks to congressional votes falling short of the constitutional requirement for a minimum two-thirds majority in both the House of Representatives and the Senate.

In the UK, by contrast, laws of a constitutional character—for example the 1998 Human Rights Act, which enshrines the European Convention on Human Rights (ECHR) into British law—enjoy no special protection. They can be amended or repealed by a simple one vote majority in the House of Commons. The Scottish and Welsh Assemblies could likewise be abolished if the UK government succeeded in mustering a single vote majority in Parliament.

The reason for this situation is that the UK constitution is founded on the principle of parliamentary sovereignty, meaning that only parliament is supreme—not the people, the judges or the monarch. Moreover, no parliament is bound by whatever was done by its predecessor. This convention explains why, after a radical change of government (from left to right, or vice versa), the incoming administration traditionally spends a substantial amount of parliamentary time repealing laws passed by its immediate forerunner.

So how did we get here? Legal experts claim that our unique constitution is a product of our specific history. Most people take the Magna Carta as the starting point. Signed in 1215 at Runnymede, not far from the River Thames and close to Windsor Castle, it was the first time that limits were placed on royal power. In this case it was King John who was brought to book, or rather to charter, by his barons. It also established basic rules for justice: 'To no one will we sell, to no one will we deny or delay right or justice … no free man is to be arrested, or imprisoned, or deprived of property, or in any way destroyed, save by the lawful judgement of his peers.'

But the big breakthrough came with the 1689 Bill of Rights, which followed the Glorious Revolution of 1688, when the unpopular Catholic King James II was effectively deposed by parliament, who then invited Queen Mary II and her Dutch Protestant husband, King William of Orange, to take the throne. But before doing so, they first had to sign the Bill of Rights, which limited the powers of the monarch and defined the rights of Parliament, including regular sessions, free elections, and free speech in the chamber.

It also set out certain individual rights, including a ban on cruel and unusual punishments, such as the gruesome fate of being hung, drawn and quartered. Two years later, the Act of Settlement confirmed Parliament's absolute supremacy and established that only Protestants could be crowned King or Queen. As a result, the British monarch reigns but does not rule, and can only come from the Protestant branch of the Christian religion.

Ironically, the Magna Carta and the English Bill of Rights inspired generations of constitution drafters worldwide—the influence of both documents can be clearly seen in the American Bill of Rights (1789), and in more recent times, the United Nations' Universal Declaration of Human Rights in 1948 and the European Convention on Human Rights in 1950. But despite having set the gold standard for codified constitutions, the UK continued to make up its own constitutional arrangements as it went along, pausing occasionally to offer advice to others, for example helping

American jurists to draft the much-admired basis for post-war Germany's Federal Republic, which now applies also to the re-unified country.

Landmark constitutional bills included the Acts of Union with Scotland and Ireland (1707 and 1800 respectively), the 1911 Parliament Act that limited the veto powers of the House of Lords, and the 1918 Representation of the People Act, which extended the vote to all men and women over 30. After the Second World War, the most significant step came in 1973 when the UK joined what would later become the European Union. A quarter of a century later, Tony Blair introduced a series of reforms which added further complexity to the UK's constitutional framework, including devolution for Scotland and Wales and the incorporation of the ECHR into domestic law.

You may be surprised to learn from the foregoing that a large part of our constitution is already written down. So technically speaking, it is not correct to say that we do not have a written constitution. Instead, what we are lacking is a codified constitution—one that includes all key elements in one document.

This approach would mean formalising hundreds of so-called conventions: rules of political practice that have evolved, often over centuries, and are generally accepted by participants in the political game. One of the most important is that the monarch always signs an act of parliament that has been passed by both chambers. Another basic rule is that, if a prime minister loses a general election, he or she resigns. Then there is the concept of collective responsibility on the part of the cabinet: government ministers are obliged to publicly support official policy, even if they personally disagree with it. If they fail to do this, or if they vote against the government in the Commons, they must resign. Under the so-called Salisbury Convention, the House of Lords never rejects or substantially delays bills that were part of the government's election manifesto. Even the prime minister's job description is a matter of convention—it does not exist in any document, legal or otherwise.

Some of these conventions are written down, but many are not, and none are legally enforceable. Instead, they are matters of tradition and interpretation, custom and practice. It was to these aspects of our nebulous constitution that the nineteenth-century journalist, historian and barrister Sir Sidney Low was referring when he made the cryptic observation that: 'We live under a system of tacit understandings—but these understandings themselves are not always understood.'[6] Two centuries later, not much has changed. In fact, the situation has become even murkier, thanks to the explosive Brexit referendum result, which one commentator referred to as 'a democracy bomb' and another as 'constitutional dynamite.'

But having the tools to handle a complicated and controversial issue like Brexit, which pitted the sovereignty of the people against the sovereignty of parliament, is just one of many reasons why we need a codified constitution. First and foremost, in a modern democracy, every citizen should have a basic understanding of the constitution. The one thing everyone can agree on is that the UK's current constitutional arrangements are opaque at the best of times (and we are not living in the best of times).

It is revealing that all but one of the six leading authorities most quoted in academic and legal discussions on the constitution were born in the nineteenth century: Walter Bagehot, A V Dicey, Sidney Low, L S Amery, Harold Laski and Ivor Jennings. The main guide to the intricacies of parliamentary procedure was written by Sir Thomas Erskine May, another venerable Victorian who was a clerk at the House of Commons. Two centuries later, why should we be delving into the arcane works of a coterie of Victorian men to shed light on the contemporary meaning of the constitution? If we need to read a series of 200-year-old guidebooks to understand our instruction manual, then we're in big trouble.

In a letter to *The Financial Times*, Alexandra Runswick, director of the Unlock Democracy campaign group, made a convincing case for the clarity that a codified constitution would bring: 'In most other countries, you can go into a bookshop and ask for a copy of the constitution. In some cases, pocket versions are given to schoolchildren to help them understand their rights. In the UK, the closest we get to this happy situation is that you can now buy pocket copies of the Magna Carta. Most people do not understand what our constitution is, and you cannot defend or uphold something you do not understand. Nor can you hold power to account when you don't know where it lies … if we are tearing up the rule book as we leave the EU and reshaping how we do things abroad, then we should also tear up the rule book at home and make this a moment of transformative change.'[7]

The second reason for a new rule book is that the current one is badly underperforming. A modern constitution should provide for a clear separation of powers between the main actors in a democracy: the executive, the legislature and the legal system. The classic example is the USA, where Congress is separate from the presidency, and organises its own affairs, including the legislative timetable and the composition of specialist committees. The president is not a member of Congress, and congressmen/women and senators do not serve in the president's administration. Presidential elections do not coincide with elections for Congress.

Contrast this with the incestuous relationship between the UK government and parliament. Not only is the prime minister a member of parliament, but he or she also controls the parliamentary timetable, as well as the membership of specialist committees. By convention, government ministers are drawn from the two houses of parliament. Far from being separated, the executive and the legislature are fused together like Siamese twins.

The absence of separation of powers engenders an equally serious constitutional failing—a complete lack of checks and balances. Provided a government can command a majority in the House of Commons, there are ultimately no limits on the power of a prime minister. In 1976, the former Conservative Lord Chancellor, Lord Hailsham, coined the phrase 'elective dictatorship.'[8] By this phrase, he meant that a government, once formed following an election victory, could proceed to dominate parliament until the next election because of the lack of effective checks and balances.

His warning was fleshed out by Princeton and Oxford University law professor Sionaidh Douglas-Scott in an article she wrote for *Prospect* magazine: 'There is, it seems, nothing that a government with a parliamentary majority may not do. It may abolish human rights legislation, reduce civil liberties, constrict the opportunities for judicial review and force through legislation against the wishes of the devolved parliaments.'[9] This threat to democracy was already foreseen in the 19th century by the constitutional theorist A V Dicey, who observed that parliamentary sovereignty was an 'instrument well adapted for the establishment of democratic despotism.'[10]

More recently, in his book, *The Last Prime Minister*, the Labour MP Graham Allen colourfully describes the unequal relationship between what he refers to as the UK Presidency and the House of Commons: 'Instead of a healthy balance, we have an executive (the UK presidency) which stands like an 800 lb gorilla alongside a wizened legislature and judiciary. They stand like cowed and malnourished dependants, the latest victims of generations of abuse accepted as normality, rather than separate, lively checks on the executive.'[11] Allen's solution is for a directly elected UK president and a much more independent and assertive parliament, along the lines of the US Congress. There is a counter argument, which can be traced back to one of the most illustrious of the Victorian thinkers cited above. Walter Bagehot, who also founded *The Economist* newspaper, maintained that the UK does not need a *separation* of powers, but rather a *balance* of powers. But, as we have seen, in normal circumstances—when the government has a working majority— there is no such thing as a balance of power at Westminster: everything is weighted in favour of the government. Parliamentary sovereignty is therefore a myth. Governmental dominion is the reality.

But you might ask, what about the King? We know he has many unusual legal privileges: for example, according to the official royal website, royal.uk, he 'retains the right to claim ownership of any unmarked mute swan swimming in open waters.' He also has first dibs on all whales, sturgeons and dolphins in the waters around England and Wales, doesn't need a passport to travel abroad, and can drive without a licence. But what about political power?

In other countries, heads of state sometimes play a key role in political events. For example, in Italy, at the height of the Eurozone crisis, Italian president Giorgio Napolitano lent his support to the ousting of prime minister Silvio Berlusconi and to the appointment of his technocratic successor, Mario Monti. The current president, Sergio Mattarella, refused to appoint a Eurosceptic finance minister even though the latter was the choice of the prime minister-designate and had the backing of a majority of parliamentarians.

Here in the UK, we have heard much about the Royal Prerogative, and it is true that, in theory, our head of state can dismiss a prime minister, refuse to sign a controversial parliamentary bill and suspend parliament. In reality, the King does what he is told by the prime minister of the day (Bagehot insisted the monarch would have to 'sign his or her own death warrant' if parliament requested it). The last time a monarch sacked a premier was in 1834, and nobody thinks it will ever happen again. Likewise, no monarch in recent history has refused to give the so-called Royal Assent to a bill that has been approved by parliament, and the power to suspend, or prorogue, parliament, is one that is exercised only at the request of the prime minister, as we saw in 2019 over Brexit.

But what the King lacks in assertiveness and power, he does, to some extent, make up for in influence. In the Netflix series *The Crown*, there is a scene where the young Princess Elizabeth is coached in constitutional theory according to Bagehot. She was quick to learn that the monarch has three essential rights: to be consulted, to encourage, and to warn. Our new King can exercise any or all of these rights in his weekly meetings with the prime minister. But, since no notes of these meetings are taken (nobody else is allowed to attend), we will never know what is discussed. In consequence, we can conclude that the monarch cannot act as a check on executive power.

However, in recent years, it has emerged that the monarch has much more power over the law-making process than was ever previously imagined. In 2021 an investigation by *The Guardian* uncovered an ancient procedural rule, applicable to the internal workings of parliament and of unclear origin, which requires the monarch's consent to be obtained for certain types of laws before they can be presented for final approval to either parliamentary chamber. Unlike the royal assent—the symbolic stamp of regal approval given to a law after it has successfully navigated both houses of parliament—King's consent gives the monarch and his advisers the opportunity to scrutinise and suggest changes to any laws that would impact on 'the prerogative ... the hereditary revenues, the Duchy of Lancaster or the Duchy of Cornwall and personal or property interests of the Crown.'

In theory, this privilege can apply to a wide range of laws, as Liverpool University's senior constitutional law lecturer, Adam Tucker, explained in *The Guardian:* 'The King pays tax, so, for example, finance laws require consent. The King is an employer, so, for example, child support and pensions laws require consent. And so on. Quite superficial connections to the interest of the Crown are sufficient to trigger the King's involvement.'[12] *The Guardian's* investigation revealed how Queen Elizabeth secretly managed to get laws changed in her favour before they were introduced. Between 1968 and 1982, the paper found four instances where the monarch had lobbied to get a law altered. For example, in 1973, Queen Elizabeth's lawyers intervened to allow her to hide her private wealth from the public.

Many take a dim view of this power to influence the laws of the land. Responding in his Guardian opinion article to reports that the Queen's advisers were even prepared on occasion to threaten to withhold consent to secure their policy preference, Adam Tucker fulminated: 'There is no place for this process in the working of a 21st-century democracy.'

Former Liberal-Democrat MP and minister Norman Baker went further, calling the practice 'a constitutional outrage' and 'a gross affront to democracy.' According to Mr

Baker: 'If an MP or peer sought to secretly influence a draft bill to advantage themselves in this way, it would be called corruption. It could lead to a criminal charge.'[13] But—despite the controversy surrounding the unearthing of King's consent—in general, the monarch does not have the constitutional means to openly challenge the power of the executive.

So, in the absence of real checks and balances, everything depends on the prime minister's personality, and how far they are willing to go to achieve their goals. Political analyst Peter Hennessy, who sits as an independent peer in the House of Lords, is credited with having invented the so-called Good Chap Theory of Government. He explained it in a paper published by the Constitution Unit of University College London (UCL):

'A key characteristic of the British constitution is the degree to which the good governance of the UK has relied on the self-restraint of those who carry it out. In the UK we have trusted politicians to behave themselves. We have long assumed that those who rise to high office will be 'good chaps', knowing what the unwritten rules are, and wanting to adhere to them. If general standards of good behaviour among senior politicians can no longer be taken for granted, then neither can the sustenance of key constitutional principles.'[14]

In recent times, the UK has experienced a series of constitutional clashes which arose when governments attempted to bend the rules to circumvent conventions. Exhibit A happened when Theresa May's government tried, without a parliamentary vote, to trigger Article 50, which would have set the clock ticking for the country's departure from the EU. Some people might see the irony in this ploy since the whole point of Brexit was ostensibly to allow parliament to take back control.

Exhibit B was when Boris Johnson asked Queen Elizabeth to prorogue parliament, in a move that was widely interpreted as an attempt to prevent MPs blocking a no-deal EU exit. In both cases, the Supreme Court ruled against the government.

Exhibit C comes from across the Atlantic. President Trump rode roughshod over many conventions that have survived for decades in US government. For example, it had previously been a convention for US presidents to publish their tax returns and distance themselves from any business interests while in office. Trump's disdain for such time-honoured customs shows that it's a simple question of power—if you have enough of it and you don't care about respecting tradition, you can override conventions. A codified constitution would prevent this danger by setting out the rules of the game in black and white, and defining their enforcement mechanisms.

In their book, *The Bonfire of the Decencies: Repairing and Restoring the British Constitution*, Andrew Blick and Peter

Hennessy warned that: 'The experience of the Johnson premiership demonstrated a fragility at the very heart of our unsystematic system, for the prime protector of the norms and procedures that animate the decencies and probity of public and political life turned out to be a wrong 'un, who repeatedly resisted the application of those very requirements to himself. In 10 Downing Street, for three whole years, they were not known at this address.'[15]

While Brexit laid bare in brutal fashion the failings of our ramshackle constitutional arrangements, the Covid-19 pandemic exposed them in a subtler way. On 10 May 2020, Boris Johnson made a televised address to the nation, to explain the next phase of the battle against the virus. His request that millions of people should return to work if they were unable to work from home was disavowed by the leaders of the three devolved assemblies in Cardiff, Edinburgh and Belfast. This led to formal checks, for the first time ever, at the border between England and Wales. Welsh police officers were deployed to turn back outsiders they suspected of wanting to enter the country for leisure or other non-essential purposes. The devolved authorities were able to flex their muscles because they are autonomous in health matters.

It turned out that the Sunday evening broadcast, which drew a record audience of 27m viewers, was made by the prime minister of England, not the prime minister of the

United Kingdom. It was a clear signal of disequilibrium in the UK's increasingly unsustainable constitutional balancing act. One of the most obvious inconsistencies is that while devolution has been extended to Wales, Scotland and Northern Ireland, the English regions have been excluded, creating an imbalance in regional democracy.

This oversight alone, argues Linda Colley, is a good enough reason for Britain to move to a codified constitution: 'The essential problem is not, as some would have it, devolution itself—but rather that this process remains seriously incomplete. No comparable, separate agency has been offered to England; and there is no thought-out federal system that would not have, as a necessary concomitant, a written constitution setting out how this system interweaves and is supposed to function.'[16]

Many now believe it is high time to call time on this half-baked federalist situation by drafting a modern constitution which defines more clearly the distribution of powers between the devolved entities and the national government. Extending devolution to the English regions should also be up for discussion.

It has been argued that constitution building is a bit like dentistry: there's never a good time for it, but it's sometimes necessary and, when it's done right, it prevents greater pain in the future. Nobody can deny we've undergone a series of major upheavals in recent years, starting with Brexit and closely followed by the pandemic and the cost-of-living crisis. It could be that our long-awaited big moment has finally arrived—it's time to book that dental appointment and get our constitutional teeth sorted out!

CHAPTER 4

PACKING IN THE PANTOMIME

Politics should be polite and boring

How could one of the world's most polite countries end up with one of the world's most unruly parliaments? International television coverage of MPs baying and braying, with the raucous wall of sound punctuated by the Speaker's exhortation of 'Order, order!', have made the House of Commons, and by extension the UK, a global laughingstock. The scenes of uproar have been variously likened to 'rival bands of warring gorillas' and 'a mass brawl at a football stadium, with MPs yelling and jeering across the field of play.' What makes such behaviour even weirder is that, in any other official UK context, it would result in severe punishment. Shouting in a courtroom can lead to a charge of contempt of court and a hefty fine. Making a ruckus in the Welsh Senedd or the Scottish Parliament would result in instant expulsion from the chamber and probably a lengthy exclusion. But rowdiness on a mass scale is somehow tolerated at Westminster, presumably because in some quaint way it is deemed to represent 'tradition.'

The eponymous author of the bible of parliamentary etiquette, Sir Thomas Erskine May, must be spinning in his Victorian grave at the shameful spats that regularly unfold at Prime Minister's Questions, or PMQs. Far from endorsing such loutish behaviour, he was a stickler for decorum, insisting that: 'Members must not disturb a member who is speaking by hissing, chanting, clapping, booing, exclamations or other interruptions.' I think we can safely assume from these words that Sir Thomas would not have been impressed by the hullabaloo-ing that is a ritual feature of high-profile parliamentary clashes. He did, however, approve of MPs giving some discreet feedback of a positive nature: 'When not uttered until the end of a sentence, the cry of "hear, hear" offers no interruption of the speech.'

But clapping after a speech is not only frowned upon, it is banned, although sometimes this rule is ignored by exuberant MPs. The reason for the prohibition is that applause could be orchestrated to give an unwarranted standing ovation, or could even be used negatively, for example through slow hand clapping. So, summing up, in our national parliament, normal social behaviour (clapping) is outlawed, while abnormal social behaviour (shouting, heckling and hurling abuse) is tolerated. If they behaved in the street like they do in the Commons, our disruptive MPs would be issued with antisocial behaviour orders (ASBOs).

This boorish behaviour by elected representatives doesn't go down well with voters. A poll carried out by Opinium for the pressure group, Compassion in Politics, found that watching PMQs and debates made 43 per cent of people lose respect for politicians, compared with just five per cent who said it increased their respect. Compassion in Politics Co-Director Jennifer Nadel slammed the booing and jeering: 'A basic rule of thumb is: if you are not allowed to do it in a classroom or a place of work you most certainly should not be allowed to do it in parliament, no matter how many years of tradition have allowed it to continue. To achieve the best outcomes for the country, we need our parliament to be the model for constructive and rigorous debate.'[1]

Have things always been this way? Not according to *The Observer's* chief political commentator, Andrew Rawnsley. He's noticed a big decline in the quality of parliamentary insults: 'Many of the giants of our political history were capable of spectacular invective. Winston Churchill once infuriated Lady (Nancy) Astor to such an extent that she said, "If I were married to you, I would put arsenic in your coffee," to which he replied: "If you were my wife, I would drink it!"' But, during the poisonous period that followed the Brexit vote, parliamentary exchanges descended into far darker territory, drawing on a sinister lexicon laced with incendiary insults such as 'treason', 'traitor' and 'surrender.'

Outside parliament, newspapers branded Supreme Court judges as 'enemies of the people,' a phrase more reminiscent of repressive totalitarian regimes than one of the world's leading democracies. Many Remain-supporting MPs received death threats, which had to be taken seriously, especially following the brutal murder of their colleague Jo Cox a few days before the Brexit referendum. Her killer, Thomas Mair, shouted 'Britain first!' before shooting and stabbing the Labour member to death. Thankfully, the political atmosphere has become less febrile and more temperate since the UK's official withdrawal from the European Union at the end of January 2020.

What explains this long-standing tolerance for parliamentary pandemonium? Part of the blame can be attributed to the design of the Palace of Westminster. The shape and configuration of the Commons chamber are physical clues that politics here is adversarial. The opposing benches encourage conflict rather than compromise. According to tradition, the front benches are two swords' length apart, marked by red lines on the carpet, so that even the fabric of the Commons' floor covering warns politicians they are only a few steps away from a real fight. The deliberate lack of seating for the full quota of MPs must also sour the mood at packed debates, with parliamentarians forced to stand for long periods, or sit awkwardly in the aisles.

Writing in *Politico,* journalist Paul Taylor believes the explanation for MPs' rude behaviour lies primarily in our history: 'Despite a global reputation for skilled diplomacy, pragmatism and common sense, the truth is that the Brits have spent centuries fighting each other and tend to regard compromise, rather than patriotism, as the last refuge of a scoundrel.'

According to his theory, conflict is in our ancestral genes: 'The UK's political culture is one of tribal confrontation, not consensus or consultation. York versus Lancaster in the Wars of the Roses; Protestants versus Catholics in more than a century of religious strife; Roundheads versus Cavaliers during the English Civil War; Whigs versus Tories throughout the 18th century; Free Traders versus supporters of the Corn Laws in the 19th century; then a century of class struggle between Labour and the Conservatives; and decades of vicious feuding between Eurosceptics and pro-Europeans.'[2]

A third factor is surely the lack of gender balance in the composition of parliament. The number of women elected to Westminster over the last century (they were legally allowed to stand as candidates in 1918) is a measly 552, compared with tens of thousands of men over the same period. Currently 225 of the 650 MPs are women, which represents a record 35 per cent of the total. Who can doubt that if these figures were reversed, with 65 per cent of women to 35 per cent of men, we would not experience the same degree of racket in the chamber?

Those noise levels reach a crescendo soon after midday every Wednesday, during prime minister's questions, when the Leader of the Opposition gets the chance to ask six questions on any subject to the man or woman running the country. Other MPs are also allowed to ask questions, both before and after the headline act. PMQs started in 1961 when Conservative prime minister Harold Macmillan faced Labour leader Hugh Gaitskell across the despatch box.

Initially it was spread over two days, with 15 minutes of questions on Tuesdays, and the same duration on Thursdays. When Tony Blair entered 10 Downing Street he compressed the two sessions into a single half hour midweek slot, and all subsequent premiers have maintained this practice. PMQs entered the public consciousness for the first time in 1978, with live radio transmissions from Westminster. But its current high-profile iteration only really took off in 1989 with the televising of parliament and the inclusion for the first time of PMQs highlights in TV news bulletins.

Both sides spend many hours preparing for this weekly showdown, which has developed into such an art form that two political aides to former Labour leader Ed Milliband have written an entire book delving into the nuances of PMQs. In the appropriately named *Punch and Judy politics—an Insider's Guide to Prime Minister's Questions*, Ayesha Hazarika and

Tom Hamilton pull no punches in defining the essence of this verbal slugfest. They say: 'It's a duel between the two main party leaders, backwards and forwards, trying to catch each other out and deliver the best jokes and rhetorical flourishes.'[3]

The main prize for finding the perfect mix of soundbite, style and wit is succinctly described by former Conservative leader, William Hague, who sparred many times with Prime Minister Blair: 'You want *The 10 O'Clock News* to say, "The PM and Leader of the Opposition had a furious argument today," and then, if they say that, that's a success, so whether you've won the argument is less important than it's a big argument.'[4]

As a spectacle, there's no doubt that these clashes liven up otherwise staid parliamentary proceedings. Some prime ministers even go so far as to defend them as a key part of our democratic tradition. For example, according to former PM, David Cameron: 'It's nerve wracking, walking into a hostile chamber, knowing you could be asked anything. But it can also be good fun. In fact, it kind of sums up British politics perfectly—a robust democracy with a sense of humour.'

But most occupants of Number 10 Downing Street loathe and dread this weekly ordeal, which forces them to rely on their wits to avoid humiliation at the hands of the person who's after their job. Even the famously unflappable Harold Macmillan, the smoothest of all Conservative operators in the 1950s, confided that he felt physically sick before

PMQs. The memoirs of another slick performer, Tony Blair, described the exchanges as 'the most nerve-racking, discombobulating, nail-biting, bowel-moving, terror-inspiring, courage-draining experience' of his political life. The public are equally unimpressed, if a Hansard Society survey carried out in 2015 can be believed. Most viewers who watched the event thought the proceedings were worse than a playground riot, with the exchanges variously described as 'pathetic,''point scoring' and 'pantomime.'

The report paints a picture of a public that is deeply dissatisfied with the culture and conduct of politics, with prime minister's questions 'a significant contributory factor in this disenchantment.' It's a view shared by John Bercow, who during his term as Commons Speaker admitted: 'There are people who think culturally the atmosphere is very male, very testosterone-fuelled and, in the worst cases, of yobbery and public school twittishness.' Former Labour leader, Ed Milliband, added: 'We should endeavour to be proud of the show we put on for the country, not giving people a sense that their kids behave better than we do.'[5]

The ultimate irony is that even stellar parliamentary performances by the leader of the opposition don't guarantee success outside the Westminster bubble. William Hague often got the better of Tony Blair across the despatch box, invariably by poking fun at the PM, only to subsequently fail miserably at the ballot box. Writing for the Institute for

Government, veteran political journalist Peter Riddell turns the argument on its head. He says a prime minister who is in a strong position nationally can easily deal with any number of brickbats from the leader of the opposition at PMQs, while a weak PM in the country is easily wounded in Commons exchanges: 'Hence, Tony Blair's famous put-down to John Major in 1995—"I lead my party, he follows his"—was effective precisely because the Conservative leader was in a weak position with a divided and fractious parliamentary party.'[6]

If PMQs don't achieve much, either in terms of overturning the political facts on the ground or of holding the government to account, why are they treated with such importance by the media? The reason could be the British addiction to politics as a branch of the performing arts. It's no coincidence that a book on the subject was entitled *Punch and Judy Politics* or that disgruntled voters often described the weekly PMQs show as a 'pantomime.'

I prefer to use the term 'politainment' for this personality-based art form. It extends well beyond Westminster, with multiple appearances by serving or recently retired politicos on such popular TV shows as *Have I Got News For You* (Boris Johnson, Jacob Rees-Mogg, Nigel Farage and Alistair Campbell, to name but a few), *Strictly Come Dancing* (most notably Ed Balls, Vince Cable, Ann Widdecombe and Edwina Curry), *I'm a Celebrity Get Me Out of Here* (Tory

MPs Matt Hancock and Nadine Dorries) and *Celebrity Big Brother* (former Labour MP George Galloway).

In October 2019, *The New York Times* journalist Alex Marshall devoted an entire article to speculation that Boris Johnson may owe his rise to fame and fortune to his appearances on the BBC's quiz show *Have I Got News For You.* According to Marshall, 'The show is mentioned repeatedly in profiles of Johnson and Rees-Mogg.' Johnson's appearances were 'pop culture classics,' wrote Sonia Purnell in *Just Boris*, her unauthorised biography of Britain's 55th Prime Minister. 'In the end his TV career may have proved his greatest electoral asset,' she added.

More anecdotally, Marshall also quotes a member of the studio audience for the iconic show: 'Emily Rayner, a civil servant standing in the queue for a recent taping of the show in Borehamwood, a commuter town north of London, said she knew people who had voted for Johnson "because they thought he's got character, (and) he's been on *Have I Got News for You.*"'[7]

Conversely, a politician who lacks the ability to entertain the public can end up paying a high price. Writing in *Prospect* magazine, Peter Chappell warned Labour leader Sir Keir Starmer to heed the fate of Jo Swinson, who went from hero to zero as leader of the Liberal Democrats in a matter of months. Comparing the two, Chappell writes:

'Swinson was a seemingly sensible choice for the Lib

Dems: competent, well qualified and good with detail. She could draw support from around the party and speak to the base. She had experience, having served as a minister in the coalition. But the more the public saw of her, the less they wanted to (support her). Starmer's similarly stiff style could torpedo his popularity with a public hungry for a political entertainer.'[8]

After extolling Starmer's track record as a human rights defender before and during a distinguished career as Director of Public Prosecutions, Chappell asks whether he can also be an effective salesman, before quoting focus groups who 'see him as corporate—easy in a room full of high-powered people. Perhaps worst of all, they describe him as 'dull.' It seems that, in the UK, the worst thing a politician can be is boring. Competence, professional knowledge and experience are shunted well down the list of job requirements and may even be tacked on the end as optional extras.

What makes this preference for entertaining politicians so peculiar is that we would never prioritise this trait in other situations. Who would you rather have as captain of your aeroplane: the pilot who tells great jokes over the intercom, or the one who came top of the class at flying school? Which dentist would you prefer to do your root treatment—the one who's a glamorous country and western singer in her spare time, or the shy one with 40 years' experience of teaching medicine as well as treating patients?

We may not be the only country to elect eccentric leaders—think Trump in the USA and Berlusconi in Italy—but most European voters put ability before affability. Angela Merkel would never have been invited onto a German comedy show. Yet this charisma-free, eminently dull Teutonic politician, whose lack of star quality makes Keir Starmer look like Jerry Seinfeld or Michael Barrymore, played a boringly key role in saving the Euro, successfully integrating one million Syrian refugees into German society and limiting the number of Coronavirus deaths to a fifth of those in the UK, despite Germany having land borders to nine countries and a population some 20 per cent bigger.

German MPs do get the chance to question their Chancellor, but it's not the rumbustious jousting contest of the Westminster kind. In any case, Germany usually has a coalition government, so the *Fragestunde* (literally 'Question Hour') is not a useful arena for the leader of the second or third largest parties, because he or she will most like already be in government as part of the coalition. Compared with PMQs, *Fragestunde* is a polite, civil and low-key affair. Questions and answers are prepared up to five days in advance and the Chancellor is not even obliged to turn up, often sending a minister instead.

Calls to liven up the occasion by making it more like the raucous midweek face-off in the Commons have been rejected. CDU whip Michael Grosse-Bromer dismissed the idea out of hand: 'Talk shows belong on television, not in a working parliament.'[9] He added that spending several hours preparing for a performance lasting 30 minutes would be a waste of the Chancellor's precious time. From Berlin, then, it's a *nein, danke* thumbs-down to PMQs.

In France, the prime minister's questions format is a non-starter because the president of the republic is not directly accountable to the *Assemblée Nationale*. The same is true of the incumbent of the White House, who has no role in congressional proceedings. In fact, among western democracies, only Australia comes close to replicating the febrile atmosphere of Westminster, occasionally even outdoing the mother country in brutal invective. Most infamously, in 2012, PM Julie Gillard told opposition leader Tony Abbott: 'If he wants to know what misogyny looks like in modern Australia, he doesn't need a motion in the House of Representatives—he needs a mirror!'

From a global perspective, it seems that subjecting the prime minister to parliamentary questions is neither an indispensable part of the democratic process, nor one that produces better outcomes in terms of policy making. On the contrary, it could be argued that sparing the PM from the hours of preparation, rehearsal and role playing that precede each weekly session would give him or her an extra chunk of time to read briefing papers and consult expert advisers on the best policy options to adopt.

But even if we cannot kick our 'politainment' habit and dispense with the weekly *Punch and Judy* show, we can surely improve the quality of the audience participation. It's a realistic prospect, demonstrated convincingly during the Coronavirus lockdown. With strict limits on the numbers of MPs allowed to enter the Commons chamber, there was a much calmer atmosphere. In the absence of the usual din, MPs who were physically present did not need to raise their voices, while those working from home were easily seen and heard. Instead of hecklers, the only interruptions to the smooth flow of proceedings were caused by technical glitches. The Speaker never needed to shout 'Order, order!'

Soon after lockdown was imposed, *Guardian* writer Richard Power Sayeed marvelled at the more polite and restrained political culture induced by the hastily improvised procedures: 'Remote working has stripped parliament of its customs and costumes. We have been confronted with the bare bones of our representative system, and the result has been overwhelmingly positive ... Wednesday's PMQs was like never before. No facile insults were screamed. There was no sonic wall of jeering ... this week our semi-digital Commons looked, for the first time in a long while, like the epicentre of a grown-up democracy—sensible and pleasingly boring.'[10]

Apart from a more collegiate and tolerant atmosphere, the so-called Zoom Parliament also introduced electronic voting, avoiding the need for MPs to vote physically, a process which involves honourable members walking into one of two rooms to get counted. It takes around fifteen minutes per division. Compare this with the chaotic—and, as it turned out, premature—restoration of the old system at the insistence of the Leader of the House, Sir Jacob Rees-Mogg.

According to Hannah White, writing in *Prospect* magazine, the slow-moving conga of parliamentarians waiting to vote with their feet didn't do anything to burnish Westminster's reputation in the eyes of the British public: 'The sight of MPs spending hours parading around the Houses of Parliament, having rejected an efficient online voting system and disenfranchising millions of voters in the process, can only erode public confidence in the politicians who are supposed to be leading them through this pandemic.'[11]

We should break decisively with the past, to restore the public's rapidly diminishing levels of trust, and either do away with PMQs completely, or, if we keep them, they should be conducted in a more civilised manner. The Commons is at least as solemn a venue as the High Court, so why should there be any difference in the rules for observing a respectful silence while somebody else is speaking?

The best solution would be to move our errant MPs into a modern parliament building, where the sober architecture would discourage bullying behaviour. That would, of course, also mean dispensing with swords lengths, woolsacks, snuff boxes, Black Rod and all the other absurdly out-dated historical baggage. But it would be a small price to pay for grown-up politics worthy of one of Europe's oldest democracies. If global Britain wants to truly earn the world's respect, it needs to get its House (of Commons) in order. It's high time for us to banish buffoonery, shun celebrity and prorogue politainment!

CHAPTER 5

LET'S GET THINGS INTO PROPORTION

Making every vote count

Let me tell you about a very special restaurant. There's nothing out of the ordinary about the quality of its cuisine. The standard of service is decidedly mediocre. The decor is nothing to write home about. But what makes this restaurant exceptional is the way you place your order. For starters (no pun intended) it only accepts large groups of diners—10 is the minimum number. What's more, each group has to order exactly the same dish, no matter what their individual tastes might be. This means that before they can order, they first have to hold a vote. Take a typical group of 10 people—there are four meat eaters, three vegetarians and three vegans. The carnivores would like the rump steak, the vegetarians prefer a lentil lasagne (made with eggs) and the vegans want a salad. In the ensuing vote, the rump steak comes out on top, with four votes, with the other two choices receiving three votes each. This means it's rump steak all round, so the non-meat eaters go home hungry. Despite the vegetarians and vegans outnumbering their carnivorous friends by six votes to four, they still lose the vote and are left eating not-so-humble (meat) pie.

Welcome to the *First Past the Post Brasserie*, the country's first (and probably last) restaurant to model itself on the nation's dubious electoral system. Although this fantasy scenario would never survive contact with reality in the commercial world, in the political universe it's the only game in town for UK national elections, despite flying in the face of traditional British values like fair play and freedom of choice.

To appreciate just how unfair the First Past the Post (FPTP) system can be, consider another theoretical example. A city council has 100 seats with 200 voters in each constituency. In its FPTP election the result is the same in every seat: 101 votes for party A and 99 votes for Party B. The result is 100 seats for Party A and zero seats for Party B, despite it receiving only 200 fewer votes than Party A (9,900 v 10,100) This is admittedly the most extreme case of what can happen under our winner-takes-all voting system, but there are plenty of real-life cases of the distorted outcomes it routinely produces.

The 2015 general election is a good example. David Cameron's Conservatives won an overall majority of 12 seats, based on a 36.9 per cent share of the total vote (on a 66 per cent turnout). The worst injustice was inflicted on the UK Independence Party (UKIP) which won 12.6 per cent of the vote—but just one parliamentary seat. Compare UKIP's meagre reward with the Scottish National Party (SNP), which sent 56 MPs to Westminster based on a modest 4.7 per cent of the national vote. The Greens, with 3.8 per cent—not far behind the SNP—ended up with only one seat. Like UKIP, the Liberal Democrats (7.9 per cent) also garnered a far bigger vote share than the SNP (4.7 per cent) but gained only eight seats. The SNP, on the other hand, benefited from the skewed FPTP system and won twice as many seats as they would have done under proportional representation (PR).

This is because FPTP favours parties whose voters are concentrated in a limited number of seats. Bedrock support for the SNP is confined to Scotland, for obvious reasons. With their vote clustered in only one part of the UK, the SNP gained one seat for every 25,972 votes cast in their favour. The Conservatives, with most of their supporters living in the south of England, needed an average 34,242 votes to win a seat. The Liberal-Democrats, with their support spread more evenly throughout Britain, required 301,989 votes per MP, nearly ten times as many as the Tories, while the Greens needed 1,157,630 votes to elect their sole parliamentarian.

Most outrageously of all, 3.8m votes for UKIP secured the party just one Westminster seat. So, the biggest losers under the FPTP system are the smaller parties. Between them, UKIP, the Lib-Dems and the Greens won nearly 25 per cent of the vote in the 2015 election. If votes and seats were aligned proportionally, they would have amassed 158 seats in the Commons. Thanks to FPTP they ended up with just 10.

Our First Past the Post system also means we are rarely governed by parties that win a majority of the popular vote. Margaret Thatcher came to power in 1979 on a 43.9 per cent vote share, which fell slightly in the elections of 1983 and 1987. Tony Blair's landslide victory of 1997 was based on 43.2 per cent of the vote. In 2005, he won an overall majority of seats with just 35 per cent of the votes. In other words, two out of three voters supported opposition parties, but they were nevertheless governed by a Labour prime minister.

You have to go back to 1935, when Stanley Baldwin's National Government Alliance won 51.8 per cent of the ballot, if you want to find a British governing party that was elected by a majority of voters.

FPTP effectively disenfranchises voters who live in so-called safe seats. These are constituencies that never change hands because the sitting MP can count on a solid bloc of loyal voters who will always outnumber the voters of any other party. Since the MP will vote consistently in parliament in support of his or her own party, constituents who didn't vote for him or her in the election will be left without any representation.

In the 2015 election, 52 per cent of all votes were cast for losing candidates. For voters in safe seats who consistently back losers, there is less and less incentive to bother to vote, because they are always on the losing side. This explains why turnout in UK general elections is generally lower than in comparably sized European democracies. While every vote counts under proportional representation, FPTP rewards only those voters who back winners.

Under FPTP, the sole group of voters with any real power to effect a change of government are those living in marginal constituencies, where the sitting MP has a slim majority and must therefore work hard to keep it. There are only a hundred or so key marginals which are heavily contested by both major parties during a general election. These so-called battleground seats with their floating (i.e. non-aligned) voters determine the outcome of the election. Opponents of FPTP are highly critical of the power the system places in the hands of the estimated 460,000 voters, or 1.6 per cent of the total, who live in key marginals.

Then Liberal-Democrat leader Tim Farron vented his frustration in the wake of the 2017 election: 'Research has shown that the result of the last election was decided by fewer than 500,000 voters in a handful of constituencies that, by mathematical accident, happened to be marginal.

That's out of nearly 40m eligible voters. That means that only one in every 80 voters actually mattered."[1]

For the 79 out of 80 voters who don't matter because they live in safe seats, there's only one alternative to seeing their vote go straight into the bin. Tactical voting is when a voter deliberately supports a candidate from a party that is not their first choice, with the aim of giving them a better chance of ousting the sitting MP. The June 2022 by-election in the Devon seat of Tiverton and Honiton is a good illustration of how tactical voting can work. In the 2019 general election the seat was won by the Conservatives with a seemingly unassailable majority of 24,239. But the seat became vacant when the incumbent Neil Parish resigned following a scandal. In 2019, Labour came a distant second, on 11,654 votes, with the Lib-Dems in third place on 8,807.

What happened in the by-election was that Labour voters tactically switched their allegiance to the Lib-Dem candidate, in the knowledge that he had the best chance of defeating the Tories. Disenchanted Conservative voters also jumped ship to the Lib-Dems. The result was one of the biggest ever by-election upsets. Thanks to tactical voting, Richard Ford turned a 24,239 Conservative majority into a Lib-Dem majority of more than 6,000, with the Tory coming second. Returning briefly to the *First Past the Post Brasserie*, the tactical voting equivalent would have been for the three vegetarians to vote for the vegan salad because that was the best way of defeating the meat eaters and avoiding the rump steak.

With so many drawbacks, you might be forgiven for wondering why Britain has persisted with FPTP for so long. Its supporters rely mainly on two arguments.

First, they say it produces stable majorities which allow a ruling party to govern decisively, without having to compromise with a coalition partner with different political priorities. However, there are a number of difficulties with this line of reasoning. The first is that in the four most recent UK elections (2010, 2015, 2017 and 2019) the system has produced only two decisive outcomes: in 2015 for David Cameron, and 2019 for Boris Johnson. So FPTP doesn't always live up to its reputation for stability.

The second problem is the implicit assumption that it's a good thing in a democracy for a party with perhaps 40 per cent of the actual vote, and possibly only a quarter of the registered vote, to lord it over opposition parties who collectively won 60 per cent of the vote, pushing through a policy programme that most of the country's citizens may oppose.

Thirdly, comparisons between the supposed stability of the FPTP system are often made with the likes of Italy, where coalitions are indeed often fragile and short-lived, rather than with models of stable government such as Germany and the Netherlands, where coalitions are robust and long-lasting. It's like warning someone never to go on a cruise because of what happened to the Titanic.

The second oft-cited advantage of FPTP is the close links it fosters between an MP and their constituents. Even prime ministers are expected by custom to hold regular surgeries in their constituencies. But these duties can sap the member's energy and distract them from their primary tasks of scrutinising draft laws and holding the government to account. Constituents often ask their MP to help them with relatively trivial matters that would be better dealt with by a social worker, councillor or the local Citizen's Advice Bureau. The most common issues are planning, housing, immigration and benefits.

Guardian journalist Juliette Jowit highlighted the negative effect on MPs of spending too much time helping constituents: 'One conscientious MP admits going to vote on legislation without having read more than the cover of the act. Another describes the embarrassment of sitting on scrutiny committees packed with colleagues who frown on anyone who asks detailed—i.e., time-consuming—questions. One describes how lack of knowledge leaves them vulnerable to capture by special interests.'[2]

But even if you believe that an MP having close links to his or her constituents is a good thing, it is not incompatible with proportional representation. For example, in Germany electors get two votes: the first for a constituency MP and the second for a party at national level. It's called the Additional Member System (AMS), and the two votes can even be cast for different parties. So German voters get the best of both worlds.

Given the obvious drawbacks of FPTP, how can we explain its staying power in British politics, other than the obvious advantages it confers on the two biggest parties and the SNP? Jess Garland of the Electoral Reform Society believes that, although we are a nation of traditionalists, attitudes are beginning to change: 'People love the tradition and I think there has been this sense for a long time that the Westminster system is the best system, it's the *Mother of All Democracies* and all that nonsense. In the last two to three years, people have started seeing the Westminster model of democracy failing before their eyes ... I think there's a growing awareness that what was traditional and established as the best way of doing things is actually antiquated and falling apart at the seams. So, there's a growing awareness that what might be familiar and traditional isn't perhaps the best way of delivering you fairness.'[3]

New Zealanders drew the same conclusion many years ago. In 1996, they dumped FPTP in favour of Germany's Additional Member System. Did this bold move result in a collapse of stability for this lamb-exporting, rugby loving former British colony? Did the country become an antip-odean tribute act to Italy's dysfunctional democracy, with an alphabet soup of political parties forming a different government every six months? Did the Kiwi economy tank, the currency plummet and investors flee for more stable climes?

The answer is an emphatic 'No.' Instead, since 1990 the country has had just five governments, compared with eight in the UK, and the economy has prospered. There has been a modest increase in the number of political parties. In 1993, the last election to be held under FPTP, there were four parties in the single chamber parliament. By 2017 they had five parties plus one independent MP. Hardly a chaotic cacophony of political voices. To quote an official British government report into the electoral experiment: 'Since 1996, New Zealand has been governed by coalitions, usually with a minority of the seats in parliament. This obviously makes it more difficult for the leading party to achieve all of its policy aims but, arguably, policy decisions reflect the views of a wider coalition of voters.'[4]

Proportional representation also works well in the UK. Some form of PR is used by each of the devolved assemblies. For Stormont elections in Northern Ireland, a PR variant called Single Transferable Vote (STV) is used. This involves ranking your preferences for the different candidates, starting with one for your first choice, two for your second, and so on. The BBC explains what happens next:

'A quota is calculated for each constituency using a mathematical formula, based on the number of seats and the number of votes cast.

'The first preference votes are all counted and any candidates who meet the quota are elected.

'If a candidate has more votes than they need to meet the quota then their extra votes are transferred to other candidates—so the candidate marked "2" on those ballot papers gets those votes instead.

'Meanwhile, the candidate with the fewest votes is knocked out and their second preferences are transferred to other candidates.'[5]

In Wales, elections for the Senedd, or Welsh Assembly, use a mixture of FPTP and the Additional Member System, so voters make two choices: one for a constituency and the second for a region. The same system is used in Scotland. Before Brexit took effect, UK elections to the European Parliament were also based on PR, with the country divided into regions where MEPs were elected based on a so-called regional list of candidates. The more votes a party gained, the more candidates from their list would be elected (except in Northern Ireland, which used the STV system). The Brexit party were the biggest winners in the last UK elections to the European Parliament, held in 2019. They won 29 seats, more than Labour and Conservatives combined.

Not surprisingly, its former leader, Nigel Farage, is an enthusiastic proponent of proportional representation. Writing in *The Daily Telegraph*, he extolled its virtues: 'The first-past-the-post system may well have been the right one to use when there were only two or three parties in contention, but in the rather more complicated 21st century, simple plurality is obviously no longer fit for purpose … If we work together, we could find the fairest system which would benefit everybody. This would be a positive way of re-energising British politics for the greater good.'[6]

In the legendary BBC comedy series, *Yes Prime Minister*, the senior civil servant, Sir Humphrey Appleby predicted that 'No PM will ever reform the electoral system. You do not kick away the ladder that got you where you are—especially while you're still standing on it!'[7]

But the prospect of Sir Humphrey having to climb down from his metaphorical ladder is growing ever stronger. A recent You Gov opinion poll showed 76 per cent of Labour party members in favour of electoral reform, with PR the most popular option. All three finalists in the 2020 Labour leadership contest said they were in favour of changing the voting system to make it more representative.

Perhaps we would be wise to listen to the counsel of a real-life Whitehall mandarin. Sir Robert Cooper held senior roles in the Foreign Office, Cabinet Office, Bank of England and the European Union. In the conclusion to his book, *The Ambassadors,* he explains the importance of solid democratic foundations to underpin a country's stability and prosperity. 'It all starts with the political system: get this right and you are more likely to get the rest right … The United Kingdom is admired for its long democratic tradition; but it has weaknesses. The strength of its traditions may even be one of them. As society changes, democracy needs to change too … One-party politics is tyranny. Two-party politics is oligarchy. Multi-party democracy is healthy. In the real world, few choices are entirely binary. Politics should be about cooperation as well as competition.'[8]

Proportional representation fits perfectly with traditional British values like fairness and non-discrimination. A country that believes in equality when it comes to ethnicity, religion, gender and sexual orientation should also believe in equality when it comes to casting a vote. In the same way that a gay person should not have to masquerade as straight, we should be able to vote for the party we sincerely support, in the knowledge that our vote will count. The very existence of tactical voting is a sign of deep democratic failure—the psephological equivalent of the canary in the coalmine. On this occasion, we need to listen to Nigel Farage, and not to Sir Humphrey. It's time to get things into proportion and admit that First Past the Post is well past its sell-by date. A case, perhaps, of playing the *Last Post* for First Past the Post.

CHAPTER 6

'NEITHER LOCAL NOR GOVERNMENT'

Our traumatised town halls

Believe it or not, Britain is the most centralised country in Europe. In sharp contrast with neighbours like France and Germany, the UK government controls 91 pence of every pound of tax revenue. The result is that London has the tightest of grips on the purse strings funding other levels of administration, including the devolved nations, local authorities and metro mayors. Power is concentrated in Whitehall and Westminster, and more specifically in the Treasury and Downing Street. This is a problem, because experience shows that in many cases, top-down decision making does not lead to optimal outcomes.

In his book, *Taking Power Back*, Simon Parker lists some of its shortcomings: 'Centrally driven housing policy has consistently failed to build enough properties to meet growing needs. Centrally managed skills policy has resulted in a mismatch between qualifications and jobs, symbolised by the oversupply of hairdressers and beauty technicians, when many firms need engineers and computer scientists'.[1] Two eminent professors of political studies, Ivor Crewe and Anthony King, wrote a voluminous book called *The Blunders of our Governments,* in which they analysed a series of well-publicised and costly mistakes made by cabinets of both main parties. They concluded that our model of centralised decision making has lost its international allure because 'today's British governments screw up so often.'[2]

One of the biggest screw-ups has resulted in the UK leading the rest of Europe, not only for over-centralisation, but also for geographical inequality of wealth and incomes. The country's richest area (the City of London) is 30 times richer than the poorest one (Ards and North Down in Northern Ireland). North of a line from the Severn estuary to the Wash, and south of Hadrian's Wall, 47 per cent of the British population lives in an area as poor as the American state of Alabama and the former East Germany. It includes the East and West Midlands, North-West, North-East, Yorkshire and Humber, Wales, and Northern Ireland.

South of that dividing line, London and the South-East have been prospering since the 1960s, with productivity per head in the capital 77 per cent higher than the national average by 2018.[3] Half of all foreign investment gravitates to London and the South-East. It's the same story for public infrastructure funding. Transport spending per head in London is £2,700 but only £5 in the North-East. Such shockingly skewed statistics might explain why a five-mile bus trip costs £1.50 in London but £5.65 in Hampshire.[4] Unlike the rest of the country, bus services in London were never privatised. Professor Tony Travers, of the London School of Economics, has described the UK's capital city as 'the dark star of the economy, inexorably sucking in resources, people and energy. Nobody quite knows how to control it.'[5] It doesn't help that some metropolitan commentators have disdainfully described London's relationship to provincial England as like being 'shackled to a corpse.'[6]

Outside London, the other obvious success story is Scotland. A generous public spending formula and the opening of the North Sea oilfields in the 1970s helped it become the third richest part of the UK. Salaries in Aberdeen and Edinburgh are the highest in the UK outside of London and the South-East. The lowest are in Sheffield, Leicester and Liverpool.

In contrast to the UK, the most equal societies in Europe tend to be those with the least centralisation. Federal Germany is a good example, with wealth and income spread between a large number of prosperous regional cities such as Hamburg, Frankfurt, Cologne, Munich and Stuttgart. Even in the relatively depressed former East Germany, the cities of Leipzig and Dresden are employment hotspots. There's plenty of evidence from Europe that decentralisation can make us richer, more equal and even happier. One study suggested that devolving more power over planning, transport and higher education to England's cities could add as much as £79bn to our gross domestic product by 2030.

Another failure of over-centralisation revealed itself during the Coronavirus pandemic. In England the vitally important test and trace system was almost entirely farmed out centrally to Serco, a large private contractor that ran its operation from call centres. In Wales a different policy decision meant the service was not outsourced, but was instead coordinated by local public health officials, ensuring that 90 per cent of contacts were traced, often thanks to boots on the ground. In the coastal area of Ceredigion, for example, this localised system helped to keep infection rates to a minimum.

By contrast, during a major outbreak in Blackburn, the privatised national tracing service reached only 52 per cent of all close contacts. Comparing the two systems at national level, local public health teams identified eight out of ten people who needed to self-isolate. But the centrally coordinated system run by Serco and another private company, Sitel, managed to identify only two out of ten isolation cases, despite receiving more than £10bn of public money. It's hard to avoid the conclusion that the private sector got the cash while the public sector delivered the goods.

According to Philip Rycroft, a former Permanent Secretary at the Department for Exiting the European Union, 'One of the really fascinating things about Coronavirus is that it has revealed just how centralised the British state still is. The way that the response has been managed has been reaching for the central solution. This in a context of a crisis which, by definition, is multi-point and where you have differences in local circumstances, differences in the response locally and where logic would have suggested that it would have been really powerful to have had more well-resourced, empowered regional actors to support dealing with this crisis. But it has revealed something fundamental about the nature of the British state, which I think does bear a lot of examination.'[7]

But an under-achieving, centralised test and trace system and stark regional differences in prosperity are just the warm-up acts for the most malign effect of over-centralisation: the hollowing out of local government, especially in England. The financial crash of 2008 led to a decade of austerity that saw local authorities lose 77 per cent of their income in the ten years to 2020, according to the Local Government Association. Many had to make draconian cuts to services to make ends meet (running a budget deficit is not an option for local authorities, which have a legal obligation to balance their books). Some councils found it impossible to square the circle created by the withdrawal of more than £16bn in central government funding.

In November 2020, Croydon became the first London council in two decades to declare itself effectively bankrupt, with a £1.5bn debt. Day-to-day control of the council was put in the hands of government commissioners. Two years earlier, Northamptonshire County Council had suffered the same fate, declaring itself bankrupt after a failed attempt to re-invent itself as a 'next generation council,' which sounds as if it was connected in some way with the TV show, *Star Trek* (actually, it was not). This process involved privatising or otherwise outsourcing its services and cutting its staff from 4,000 to 150. Enterprising it might have been, but as Dr McCoy would surely have remarked to Captain James T Kirk, had the star fleet duo beamed themselves down to the Tory flagship council's Northampton headquarters: 'It's local government, Jim, but not as we know it.'

Similarly, Slough Council in the Thames Valley effectively went bankrupt after it tried to make money by property speculation, which included buying a cinema in Basingstoke. It is not known if the picture-house ever showed a *Star Trek* movie, but council tax bills were beamed up by nearly 10 per cent in just one year. And, sadly, the authority has been forced to sell an historic former cinema in Slough, where the Beatles performed in the 1960s.

Slough was just one of many English councils—Croydon was another prime example—which attempted to offset the spending cuts imposed by central government by embarking on an investment spree that saw them shell out £6.6bn from 2016-19, according to the public spending watchdog, the National Audit Office. Their acquisitions included commercial property such as office buildings and shopping centres, but also businesses, from renewable energy producers to start-up banks.

Conservative-controlled Spelthorne district council in Surrey was one of the pioneers. Using cheap, Treasury-backed loans, it built up a £1bn real estate portfolio to generate rental revenue that it hoped would offset £2.5m of cuts in government grants. It claimed that income from commercial property would cover half of its £22m annual operating budget, raising more revenue than the council tax, thereby avoiding cuts to meals on wheels services and less frequent bin collections.

Opposition councillors accused it of 'gambling with residents' money' but leader Ian Harvey told *The Financial Times* that his critics were 'devoid of realistic alternatives' to government cuts to its central grant funding.[8]

Another Conservative-controlled authority, Barnet, adopted a different strategy. It was dubbed the easyJet council after announcing plans to get some people to pay more for extra services, with a no-frills provision for everyone else. Just as easyJet and Ryanair passengers pay a premium for choosing their seats and being fast-tracked through airport security, Barnet offered to fast-track planning applications in return for an extra payment. Council leader Lynne Hillan justified the move by citing examples from other sectors: 'If you want a passport to arrive faster you pay more—and no one objects to the extra cost of a first-class stamp. People should have a similar choice with public services. So, if a resident said 'I don't need to fill a large bin, I will have a smaller bin and recycle more', we could give them a council tax discount.'[9] But Tony Travers from the London School of Economics pointed out that this approach could not be applied to all council services: 'How can you say you will sweep more carefully outside someone's house if they pay extra?'.[10]

Labour-controlled Lambeth drew inspiration from a contrasting private sector business model. It became known as the John Lewis council when it revealed plans to become a co-operative. While the department store makes partners of its staff, who share in its profits, Lambeth's idea was to encourage residents to take part in regeneration projects, in return for a council tax rebate. The council's leader at the time, Steve Reed, explained that some things could be managed more cost effectively by the community: 'For example, imagine you have a piece of waste ground which you want to tidy up. Instead of the council doing it, you give the community the tools and neighbours do it for themselves. Instead of costing several thousand pounds, doing it that way will cost only £300 and in addition, the community gains a sense of ownership of the space, and people get to know each other better.'[11]

But, despite these isolated experiments to keep metaphorical council heads above water, across the country—particularly in England—the impact of a decade of austerity is all too evident: pot-holed roads, sporadic bin collections, moth-balled libraries, shuttered swimming pools and leisure centres, abandoned parks and bus services slashed at the same time as fares are spiralling. Liverpool has been among the worst-hit. In May 2018, its elected mayor Joe Anderson told *the New European's* Peter Hetherington that, even if the council closed every one of its 19 libraries and nine of its leisure centres, stopped maintaining its 140 parks, abandoned road maintenance and street cleaning and turned off 50,000 streetlights, it would still only save about £68m—£22m short of the savings it had to make by 2020.[12]

The national picture is no prettier than this depressing snap-shot from Merseyside. Nearly 800 libraries have closed since 2010, representing almost a fifth of the total. Birmingham's magnificent central library—which cost £189m to build and won worldwide critical acclaim for its stunning architecture and state-of-the-art digital information resources—is currently only open for 40 hours a week, as the city struggles to make ends meet.

During the same decade of austerity, more than 700 youth centres were closed, while one in three of those that survived were facing the same fate by June 2021. Many councils, including Manchester, now manage only one public toilet among their other services, while some authorities, including Newcastle, have no public conveniences at all. Pinching pennies, rather than spending them, now seems to be the universal priority for cash-strapped local authorities. But it is the public who are inconvenienced, in more ways than one.

Writing in the *London Review of Books*, Tom Crewe warned in apocalyptic terms of the wider dangers of prolonged austerity: 'We fret and fume about this council here, that service there, while the whole system is sliding off a cliff. There are hundreds of local examples of the impact of austerity, each unhappy in its own way, but it is only when they are viewed in aggregate that a picture emerges of an entire social infrastructure being destroyed. Local government has been divested of much of its power and independence, leaving the gap between the public and their government to be bridged by private companies, if at all. The institutions that sustained a progressive municipal view of the world have been destroyed. The last relics of the expansive, care oriented state are being shredded.'[13]

The Guardian's John Harris makes a different point, in the context of the UK's departure from the European Union: 'Whatever the talk at the top about some imagined post-Brexit national rebirth, you won't unleash the creativity of people in disadvantaged places if their most basic services are in constant decline.'[14]

So how did it come to this? Things looked very different in the 19th century when the modern form of local government first took root. In 1873, a successful businessman and former Sunday school teacher named Joseph Chamberlain was elected mayor of Birmingham, standing as a Liberal. He pioneered what became known as municipal socialism, or gas and water socialism. By taking over the provision of gas and water from private companies, the council used the resulting profits to improve the city in numerous ways, from clearing slums and replacing them with modern, local authority-owned housing, to developing a network of trams, and later, buses—while setting up well-stocked libraries that were the envy of the rest of the country. For mid to late Victorians there was nothing so important as transforming the built environment to improve both the physical health and moral habits of its inhabitants. Polluted water, crowded and dirty homes, and poorly ventilated streets not only fostered disease, they also produced crime, domestic violence and intellectual stagnation. In 1890, the American writer Julian Ralph described Birmingham as 'the best governed city in the world.'[15] Like so many others, he was impressed not only with the quality of its institutions, but also with the capabilities of the officials.

In the 20th century, it was the London borough of Bermondsey that blazed a trail for popular and effective local government. Chamberlain's London counterpart was Dr

Alfred Salter, the council's Labour leader in the 1920s and 30s. Under his dynamic leadership, there was an energetic campaign of works to improve the health and living conditions of the mainly working-class population. A greening of the borough took place, with trees planted in nearly every street, a proliferation of flower beds and the development of open spaces for recreational use.

All this was supervised by the appropriately named Beautification Committee. A garden city was built by demolishing two thirds of the borough's substandard housing. Perhaps most impressive of all was a drive to eradicate tuberculosis. The programme included the provision of tuberculosis-tested milk while sending stricken residents to Switzerland to recover in a sanatorium, before a unit was eventually built in the borough. A state-of-the-art swimming pool and a free public library were designed to encourage the health of citizens in body and in mind.

Such was the range of provision on offer during this golden age of municipal socialism that in 1930 an MP observed that, 'A young person today lives in a municipal house, and he washes himself in municipal water. He rides on a municipal tram or omnibus, and I have no doubt that before long, he will be riding in a municipal aeroplane. He walks on a municipal road; he is educated in a municipal school. He reads in a municipal library, and he has his sport on a municipal recreation ground. When he is ill, he is doctored and nursed in a municipal hospital and when he dies, he is buried in a municipal cemetery.'[16]

Bermondsey was not the only hotbed of municipal socialism during this period. The Labour mayors of Stepney, Hackney and Poplar were respectively Clement Attlee, Herbert Morrison and George Lansbury, who all later became leading national politicians, and in Attlee's case, prime minister. This is indeed ironic, because the landslide Labour victory of 1945 that ushered in the foundation of the modern welfare state also carried with it the seeds of decline for municipal socialism and the all-encompassing role of local government in the lives of British people.

In particular, it was the wave of nationalisations that followed Labour's victory that dealt a hammer blow to municipal independence. Council-owned gas, water and electricity companies and their profits were now transferred to central government, depriving councils of a huge slice of their independent income. The creation of the National Health Service led to the nationalisation of municipal hospitals. In the case of Bermondsey, which had developed some of the highest-quality healthcare in the country—thanks to higher property taxes that most of its residents were happy to pay—health provision now had to be *reduced* so it conformed with the *lower* national standards of an NHS that was funded centrally from income tax receipts, instead of locally by rate- (property tax-) payers. As time passed, local authorities found themselves increasingly reduced to mere agents of the centralised welfare state.

As well as losing its financial independence and becoming the servant and supplicant of the Treasury and Downing Street, local government's very identity came under attack with frequent and extensive boundary and administrative changes imposed from 1972 onwards. In Scotland, traditional counties were abolished en masse, to be replaced by nine regions with 53 districts. In England, small counties like Westmorland and the divisions of Lincolnshire disappeared, while others, like Hereford and Worcestershire, were merged into a single county. In Wales, 13 counties were combined into eight units with little in the way of common cultural identity. English-speaking Pembrokeshire was merged with Welsh-speaking Cardigan and Carmarthen to form Dyfed, a name unfamiliar to most Welsh speakers, let alone Anglophones.

The meaningless names given to the new authorities symbolised the loss of local identity that these reorganisations invariably involved. In their book, *Centralisation, Devolution and the Future of Local Government in England,* authors Steve Leach, John Stewart and George Jones argue that the labels were deliberately invented to allow councils to begin afresh with an entirely new identity, reminiscent of the witness protection programme portrayed in American gangster films.

The writers explain that the artificial names can be divided into three categories. First, there are the 'compass point councils' whose names suggest they are designed to help orient travellers not equipped with satellite navigation devices. Examples are South Norfolk, West Berkshire, East Northamptonshire and North Kesteven. One district council gets bonus compass-point points: North East Derbyshire. The second category is the 'non-existent councils' whose names are simply made up without any authentic local roots. These include Three Rivers, Calderdale, Havering, Tameside, Trafford, Sefton and Sandwell. Another example, Kirklees, derives tenuously from Kirklees Priory, where Robin Hood is rumoured to be buried. Presumably, the council's staff are a merry band of men and women. Finally, there are the 'and' councils, unimaginatively lumping together the names of the merged authorities. So, we have Kings Lynn and West Norfolk, Oadby and Wigston, and Epsom and Ewel. The list goes on ad nauseam.[17]

Mergers like this have led to increasingly large units of local government, especially in England. While the average European municipality has a population of 10,000, in the UK the average district is more than ten times as big, while most English metropolitan boroughs have around 300,000 residents. A unitary county authority can have up to 1m inhabitants. Professor Colin Copus, the emeritus professor of local politics at De Montfort University in Leicester, believes such huge units inevitably result in a disconnection between the authority and the people it represents.

He goes even further by describing local government in England as neither local nor government. The local part of his argument rests on the size issue, which he says makes a mockery of any concept of 'localism.' The government part of his analysis is based on the lack of autonomy and protection afforded to local councils against interference from central government: 'If you can't pass local legislation, you're open to being abolished and merged, you're controlled heavily by the centre, 80 per cent of your finances come from two sources, both of which are heavily controlled by the centre, how can you call yourself government? You don't have any of the criteria of the dictionary definition.'[18]

The solution, according to Professor Copus and many others, is to enshrine local government's right to exist, ideally in a codified constitution. But, within the limits of the UK's existing informal system, the next best thing would be a quasi-constitutional statute. Many other countries, including the USA, have already taken this step. Any proposed boundary changes to an American local authority area have to be put to a referendum, which invariably results in the plan being rejected.

The flip side of having Europe's largest local government authorities is that the UK has a very small number of councillors—just 20,000 for the whole of England. In contrast, France has more mayors (35,000) than the UK has councillors. When it holds nationwide local elections, 500,000 council seats are up for grabs. This is because France has more than 35,000 communes, most of which trace their roots back to parishes from pre-revolutionary times. Some of them have fewer than 1,000 inhabitants. This translates into better representation at local level: in France, there is one local authority member for every 118 people, compared with one councillor for every 2,603 inhabitants in the UK.

It is clearly more expensive to have greater numbers of representatives. However, research suggests that, in the long run, the process may lead to savings—resulting from more effective policy making and a better use of resources. It's argued that councillors who have closer contact with residents are more likely to have a deeper understanding of their problems and priorities. Studies from Denmark, the Netherlands, Norway and the UK conclude that the smaller the council, the more trust citizens have in their elected representatives, and the more likely they are to vote in local elections.

Many councillors complain of the disdain in which they say they are held by Whitehall and Westminster. They believe national civil servants act as if they are superior to their counterparts in local government, while MPs look down on councillors. A widely held opinion in London's corridors of power is that councillors are generally of a poor calibre. This ingrained prejudice is believed by many in local government to be one of the main motives behind the relentless drive towards increasing the number of unitary authorities, which entails merging several councils into one authority, resulting in a reduction in the number of elected members. According to some experts, it's an exercise in culling the herd, in the hope that those who survive will be of higher quality. Perhaps more importantly, claim critics, the fewer the number of authorities, the easier they are to control from the centre.

Labour Councillor John Warmisham, from Salford, told me of his frustration with London's lack of appreciation for the work carried out at local level by elected representatives from all parties. 'Central government needs to respect local government because that respect has not been there for a long time. I've been a councillor for 30 years and I love the work and the people I represent. But you get no recognition: you feel like you're just a nuisance for central government. And that needs to change, because, ultimately, local politics affects people's lives, every day of their lives. Local government has been undermined and demeaned right back to Thatcher. The last politician who really understood local government was James Callaghan.'[19]

In other European countries, local government is taken much more seriously at national level because it is a proven training ground for leaders aiming to make it to the top of the 'greasy pole' of national politics. In France, for example, mayors often use their local power base as a launch pad for a glittering political career in Paris. Under French law, they can keep their job as mayor while working in the capital. One recent high-profile example was President Macron's first prime minister, Edouard Philippe, (mayor of Le Havre) who became so popular that he was eventually replaced by a less charismatic figure. Bordeaux mayor, Alain Juppé, was President Chirac's prime minister, while Martine Aubrey, the mayor of Lille, was minister of labour in the cabinet of Prime Minister Lionel Jospin.

Such figures leverage their national profile to bring major infrastructure projects to their cities. This may explain why France's second, third and fourth biggest cities have eight underground lines between them (four in Lyon, two each in Marseille and Lille) while their UK equivalents, Manchester, Birmingham, and Leeds, have none. It's a slightly more positive story for tram lines. Manchester and Lyon have similar-sized tramway systems, with about 100 stations each. But Marseille (three tram lines) and Lille (two) substantially outdo Birmingham (one line) and Leeds, which has no lines at all: with a population of nearly 500,000, the latter is the largest European city without a mass transit system.

In Germany, Angela Merkel's successor as chancellor was Armin Laschet, who was elected leader of the Christian Democrats (CDU) in January 2021 thanks in large part to his prominent role as prime minister of the country's most populous state, North-Rhine Westphalia. (Laschet was, however, replaced as CDU leader by Friedrich Merz after their party lost power in the parliamentary elections of September 2021).

By contrast, in England the leading metro (city-region) mayors tend to be drawn almost exclusively from the ranks of MPs. Sadiq Khan (London), Andy Burnham (Manchester) and Dan Jarvis (Sheffield) are current examples from the Labour benches. On the other side of the aisle, Boris Johnson is a rare example of a politician going in the opposite direction, from mayor of London to foreign secretary and then prime minister (though, like Ken Livingstone and Sadiq Khan, he was an MP before becoming mayor of London). But Johnson was never a ward councillor, and fewer and fewer MPs have grassroots experience in local government.

Another contrast with local government on the other side of the English Channel is election turnout. At 35 per cent, the UK has one of the continent's lowest voter participation rates. In Europe, the average 66 per cent participation rate is nearly twice as high as the UK. After a particularly poor turnout in the May 2003 council elections, *The Observer* remarked that more votes had been cast in the previous series of the *Big Brother* TV reality show.

The prime suspect for the UK's voter apathy problem is the First Past the Post (FPTP) voting system, which, in 2011, allowed Conservatives in Bournemouth to scoop nearly 90 per cent of the seats with just 38.6 per cent of the votes. In the same elections, the Lib-Dems took all of the available seats in Eastleigh with a 46.9 per cent share. Maybe not quite up to North Korean standards of distorted electoral outcomes, but a respectable attempt, nonetheless.

Research suggests that another cause of voter apathy is the large number of uncontested seats. Removing any choice at all disenfranchises and de-motivates voters in the wards concerned. Even if the winning party in a particular seat is a foregone conclusion, voters are surely entitled to be offered a choice of candidates from within that party. Overlong incumbency is another major bugbear. This problem could be easily overcome by imposing time limits on elected members, but that would penalise popular councillors from standing again. Instead, there should be moves to encourage competition between candidates, both within parties and between them. However, as Sir Humphrey remarked, there is little motivation for those in power to trash a system in which they have spectacularly succeeded.

One of the best ways to boost voter turnout and energise political activism at local level would be to introduce the Single Transferable Vote (STV) system. It is already used for local elections in Scotland, and has been a common fixture of municipal elections for many years in mainland Europe. This approach allows voters to rank their choices in order of preference in multi-member constituencies. The arrangement encourages competition within and between parties. It also means that many more voters get to see their first preference candidates elected, and overall, there are very few wasted votes.

Apart from dumping the FPTP polling system in favour of STV, how can Britain, and more especially England, reverse the tide of centralisation and rediscover its original flair for local democracy? One source of inspiration is another remarkable Victorian from Birmingham (though he is far less famous than Joseph Chamberlain). Born in 1816, Joshua Toulmin Smith was a polymath who trained as a barrister but was also an authority on subjects as varied as philosophy and geology. He believed passionately in local self-government as the best way of ensuring maximum freedom for the individual, by allowing the fewest possible number of people to directly participate in the smallest unit of government to take decisions on matters of collective concern.

Politically conservative, he argued that England's local government tradition could be traced back to the Anglo-Saxons, citing as proof William the Conqueror's *Domesday* book, which inventoried the realm's property in the aftermath of the Norman Conquest. A co-founder of the Anti-Centralisation Union, Smith would certainly have approved of the European Union's 'subsidiarity' principle, which recommends that power should be passed down to the smallest political unit capable of undertaking the required public function.

It's a value that is also enshrined in a refreshingly concise, clear and inspirational international treaty, which Great Britain signed in 1997, and ratified the following year. (Strangely, it does not apply to Northern Ireland. The explanation may lie in the date, which coincided with a sensitive stage in the peace process, which led to the Good Friday Agreement in 1998). The European Charter of Local Self-Government is still applicable in England, Wales and Scotland, since its non-EU origins mean it is wholly unaffected by Brexit.

It was drafted instead by the Council of Europe, the Strasbourg-based democracy and human rights organisation. The UK's wartime prime minister, Sir Winston Churchill, was one of an illustrious band of post-war European leaders behind its foundation in 1949, fully eight years before the Treaty of Rome that marks the birth of what later became the European Union. The Council of Europe currently comprises 46 member states, including the UK and countries as diverse as Ukraine and Turkey.

Most famous for its European Court of Human Rights, the Council also promotes local and regional government, hence the afore-mentioned European Charter of Local Self-Government, which reads like a wish list of sound principles for allowing citizens to take back control at local level.

Article Two, for example, commits signatory states to

recognising the principle of local self-government in domestic law, and, if possible, in the constitution. In other words, Britain should legally enshrine the right of local government to exist, a key goal for supporters of local democracy. Article Five says local communities should be consulted on proposed changes to council boundaries, preferably by referendum. This would greatly limit the scope for centrally driven re-organisations to create ever-larger units of municipal government. Article Nine covers the crucial question of how local government should be financed. It states that adequate resources should come from diverse local sources, with access to capital markets to fund investment projects.

To sum up: if we are serious about revitalising local government in the UK, and especially in England, it will require bold and radical steps to let power flow from the centre to the grassroots, in accordance with principles such as small is beautiful and think big, act local. Many national reforms advocated in previous chapters, including a codified constitution and a truly representative voting system, would also greatly benefit local democracy. But fully implementing the European Charter of Local-Self Government would be the game-changer. In so many ways, it would give real meaning to the Brexit-inspired *take back control* slogan. The risks of inaction have been eloquently expressed by *The Guardian* journalist John Harris, who, for more than a decade, has travelled across the UK asking ordinary people for their opinions, for the award-winning video series, *Anywhere but Westminster:*

'Just about every aspect of our current national impasse proves that the old, centralised game is up, and that England needs a new constitutional settlement. This does not strike me as a left/right issue, unless you are the kind of Tory who thinks that the neglect and outright destruction of local government ought to be a necessary part of your politics. Power needs to be taken from the centre and dispersed: the future needs to be founded on a huge boost to councils' share of the tax take, the devolution of everything from health to transport, and fully localised responses to any future emergencies. If we do not begin this revolution soon, we will carry on bumbling from one crisis to another, as Whitehall and Westminster fall into more scandal and disgrace and the commands barked from on high continue to fade into white noise.'[20]

CHAPTER 7

DON'T MENTION THE EMPIRE

Confronting Britain's colonial past

In the legendary BBC television comedy series *Fawlty Towers*, an episode entitled *The Germans* features John Cleese's manic hotelier Basil Fawlty riling a group of German guests with a series of tasteless references to the Second World War.[1] Despite one victim bursting into tears, Fawlty continues his xenophobic rant by reprising the *Monty Python Ministry of Silly Walks* routine, but this time in a more sinister incarnation as a Nazi goose-step, before berating the guests for lacking a sense of humour. The sketch is punctuated by Fawlty reciting to himself, sotto voce, the mantra *Don't Mention the War!* This sentence has since become a popular catchphrase in Britain, often used to refer to other sensitive subjects best avoided in polite conversation.

The great irony in all of this is that, for many decades, the Germans have felt it their duty not only to keep mentioning the war, but to teach it systematically to their children. The rise of the Nazi party, the Holocaust, and the devastating conflict that led to the defeat of fascism and the birth of modern Germany, are compulsory elements of the German national education curriculum. School visits to former concentration camps are encouraged. In many cities, there are small brass plates, the size of cobble stones, embedded in pavements outside the homes of Jewish Holocaust victims, bearing their names and the date when they were taken away, never to return.

When I moved in 1996 to Strasbourg, a French city bordering Germany, I was amazed to see German television still screening British and American Second World War films produced in the 1960s and 70s. The titles, including *The Battle of Britain, Where Eagles Dare,* and *The Guns of Navarone*, depict the Allies as heroes and the Germans as villains. Such films had long disappeared from British TV screens, but there was still an appetite for them in Germany, illustrating the latter country's enduring desire to confront and come to terms with its recent past. Perhaps, most tellingly, in the post-war period, Germany has paid nearly €80bn euros to victims of the Nazis, with a substantial proportion of the compensation going to the state of Israel.

Compare the German approach to the Nazi era with the British attitude to its empire, which covered 24 per cent of the earth's surface and had more than 400m inhabitants at its territorial height. Britons proudly called it the empire on which the sun never set, because— no matter what time of day it was in London—there was always light in a British colony somewhere on the planet. But the biggest empire the world has ever seen is strangely absent, not only from our education system, but also from many key national events. The spectacular opening ceremony for the 2012 London Olympics made no reference to the empire, except obliquely in one sequence which featured the *Empire Windrush*, the ship that in 1948 brought more than 1,000, mostly Caribbean, people to the UK, and which, decades later, gave its name to a scandal that exposed the denial of basic citizenship rights by the British state to many of those who arrived in the post-war years.

When people apply for British citizenship, they are tested on their knowledge of key moments in British history and culture. Yet, in the Home Office materials given to applicants to prepare for the test, there is little mention of the empire. Far more space is devoted to the First and Second World Wars. That's a curious emphasis, according to *The Financial Times* columnist, Gideon Rachman. He observed that: 'For a Martian historian, the most interesting thing about modern British history would surely be that the country built a massive global empire.'[2]

When Salman Rushdie visited Strasbourg a few years ago to promote his latest book, he told the audience of his disgust that his two sons, both educated in the UK, had received 'not one hour of teaching about the British Empire.' What lies behind this extraordinary national amnesia? How come German children are obliged to learn about the darkest period of their history, while British children can at best study their country's greatest achievement as an option, and at worst are denied any knowledge of it at all? (Such was my case at a Welsh comprehensive school in the 1970s). Internationally, this makes us an imperial outlier—my Greek colleagues tell me that Ancient Greece and Alexander the Great were an integral part of their education, and you can be sure that Italian schoolchildren are obliged to learn all about the Roman Empire.

Returning to *Fawlty Towers,* there's a delicious double irony in the notorious '*Germans*' episode. Not only does it paint a completely false picture of German sensitivities about the Second World War and all that preceded it, but it turns out that the country that is making a deliberate effort to forget a major period of its history is not Germany but Basil Fawlty's United Kingdom. A case, perhaps, of *Don't Mention the Opium Wars?*

There are three main reasons why the British Empire is discreetly brushed under the carpet. First, it all happened overseas, which is a handy justification for history teachers to concentrate on events that took place in Britain, and particularly in England. Writing for *The New York Times,* Benjamin

Mueller quotes a British doctor who lamented the lack of empire history teaching at his school: 'We're taught about the Wars of the Roses and Henry VIII's wives. And then nothing happened, and Britain did the Industrial Revolution, beat the Nazis and Churchill saved everything.'[3] The history of the British in India is transformed into Indian history and what we did to China is taught to Chinese children but rarely to their British counterparts. Teaching our foreign past is thus outsourced to the countries where it took place, and quietly erased from our national consciousness by giving it a low to non-existent profile in our domestic curriculum.

The second reason for the cloak of imperial invisibility is that it is closely associated with the Atlantic slave trade, which between 1660 and 1807 saw around 3m Africans transported to the Americas. In his book *Empireland,* Sathnam Sanghera describes the conditions on board the ships: 'The slaves kept shackled to each other or to the deck to prevent mutiny during the middle passage, stacked in tiers, with no space to turn, the dysentery, suicides, epidemics and murders killing so many Africans on the way that sharks frequently pursued slave ships on their journey west. Over this extended period, Britain was dehumanising black people on an industrial scale.'[4]

Unsurprisingly, perhaps, for a country reluctant to look its history in the eye, the focus in UK schools is on Britain's achievement in abolishing slavery, rather than on its role as a systematic abuser of human rights for the preceding 150 years. There was equal shame in the abolition settlement itself, which saw the slave owners amply compensated for the loss of their human chattels, but no compensation whatsoever paid to the victims of slavery. Such was the mammoth scale of the compensation deal (equivalent to £17bn in today's money) that British taxpayers—many of them the descendants of slaves—were still paying off the Crown's debt up until 2015. While Germany paid reparations to the victims of Fascism, Britain rewarded the perpetrators of one of the greatest crimes against humanity in world history. It's easy to understand why it's better for our sense of national self-esteem to keep the focus on our role in fighting Fascism from 1939 to 1945 instead of learning more about what we have in common with the Nazis.

The third and, perhaps, most important reason for downplaying the empire is that we did some exceedingly nasty things to the people we subjugated. Don't mention the 1919 Amritsar massacre, in which at least 379 men, women and children were shot dead by Gurkhas under the command of a British officer, as the Indians protested peacefully against British rule. He ordered the soldiers to keep firing until they ran out of ammunition. Winston Churchill described the incident as monstrous. Don't mention either the nearly 30m Indians who died of starvation while their country was run by the British, who preferred to export Indian wheat instead of using it for famine relief in the sub-continent. In 1943 alone, 3m Bengalis starved to death after Churchill diverted their food to support the war effort. He later said: 'I hate Indians. They are a beastly nation with a beastly religion. The famine was their own fault for breeding like rabbits.'[5]

Better keep quiet too about the thousands of Kenyans mistreated, raped, and tortured by British forces during the Mau Mau rebellion in the 1950s. Among those who suffered was Barack Obama's paternal grandfather. Hussein Onyango Obama fought for the British army in Burma, but, after he returned to his native Kenya, he was imprisoned and tortured by his former paymasters, leaving him with permanent scars, both physical and mental. Estimates of deaths in Kenya, at the hands of the British, range from 20,000 to 100,000.

Elsewhere in Africa the UK yoke was no less cruel. During the Second Boer War, from 1899 to 1902, British soldiers rounded up around a sixth of the population, mainly women and children, and kept them undernourished in overcrowded concentration camps prone to outbreaks of disease. Nearly 28,000 Boers died, together with an unknown number of black Africans. Closer to home, 14 civilians were shot dead at a Gaelic football match in Dublin in 1920 by British forces incensed by a series of IRA assassinations in the city. The incident, which became known as the original Bloody Sunday (there would be a second one in

Londonderry, 52 years later), greatly increased public support for Irish independence.

Between 1967 and 1973, the UK deported thousands of Chagos islanders from their idyllic Indian Ocean archipelago to make way for an American military base on the island of Diego Garcia. They were mainly sent to Mauritius and the Seychelles, but some ended up in the UK. In one incident on 24 April 1973, 400 people were rounded up and given 24 hours to pack their possessions into a single trunk. They were forced to leave behind not only their homes and land, but also their pet dogs, which were then poisoned or gassed to death by the British authorities. Britain lost several legal cases at the United Nations but has refused to recognise Mauritius's claim to sovereignty over the islands, which would allow the Chagossians to return to their homeland, the last British colony in Africa (although, according to international law, it is an illegal occupation).

The word 'loot' has Hindi origins, and for good reason. Britain looted India to the tune of $45tn dollars in today's money. That's 17 times more than the UK's current total annual gross domestic product. Men like Robert Clive made huge fortunes from their exploits on the subcontinent. The railways—often cited as Britain's generous contribution to India's economic infrastructure and in recent years the subject of endless television documentaries—were built with two main aims: to speed up troop movements around the vast country, and to facilitate the export of raw materials. In neighbouring China, the British went to war to force the Chinese to import opium grown in India, sales of which allowed the British to pay for Chinese tea, silks and porcelain.

George Orwell, the author of *1984* and *Animal Farm,* had a personal connection to the trade. His father worked for the Indian Civil Service in the department responsible for growing and processing opium destined for China. How many UK citizens are aware that their country (which still criminalises cannabis) was once a narco state profiting from the sale of hard drugs at the point of a gun? Empire was about many things, but foremost among them were conquest and commerce. So maybe it wasn't such a bad idea after all to leave empire out of that London Olympic Games opening ceremony. It might have prompted some painful memories for athletes representing the countries we occupied.

It's been calculated that Britain conquered or invaded at least 90 per cent of the 193 member states of the United Nations. For hundreds of years, our national prosperity was built on imperial aggression, oppression, and exploitation. The renowned Indian textile industry was destroyed in order to boost the growth of its British rival. According to Dr Sascha Auerbach, a lecturer in modern British and colonial history at Nottingham University, 'Britain made little effort to develop modern industry in its colonies, preferring to keep them as suppliers of raw materials and markets for commodities made in Britain.' Meanwhile, profits from the slave trade financed the development of cities like Bristol, Glasgow and Liverpool, as well as the construction of hundreds of elegant town houses and sumptuous country mansions, many of which are now owned by the National Trust.

Yet, despite all the evidence, many Britons continue to feel nostalgic about the empire. A YouGov poll carried out in 2014 found that 59 per cent of those questioned thought that the British Empire was 'something to be proud of.' Only 19 per cent claimed to 'be ashamed' of its misdeeds, and more than 30 per cent claimed, 'they would like it if Britain still had an empire.' A later poll, in January 2016, also by YouGov, found that 44 per cent of Britons believed that their country's 'history of colonialism' was something to be proud of, and 43 per cent deemed the British Empire to be 'a good thing.' More recently, in March 2020, YouGov found that 30 per cent of Britons thought former colonies were better off as part of the British Empire.[6]

On television and in cinemas, lavish costume dramas like *The Jewel in the Crown, Heat and Dust, A Passage to India*, and more recently *Indian Summers* glamourise the British Raj, while TV documentaries seek to portray the benign nature of British rule by extolling the virtues of India's railways. In London, swish Indian restaurants with imperial-period decor and evocative names like *Gymkhana* and *Veeraswamy* are all the rage—or should that be all the raj? In perhaps the most tasteless example of colonial re-branding, there is even a chain called the 'East India Company', which sells tea.

The same heady mix of amnesia and nostalgia applies to Britain's attitude to the Second World War. More than any other period in history, our national identity is bound up with this conflict. Our role in defeating Fascism seems to be our national get-out-of-jail-free card for expiating the sins of empire. We may have invaded scores of countries and turned them into vassal states, but we not only successfully resisted Nazi attempts to give us a taste of our own medicine, we also went on to help liberate Western Europe from the German yoke. In its citizenship test, the Home Office sets great store on applicants understanding the terms 'the Blitz spirit' and the 'Dunkirk spirit' and being able to quote from famous Churchillian speeches designed to stiffen national resistance to the Nazi threat.

In yet another irony, prospective citizens who do their homework for the test will end up knowing far more about the realities of the Second World War than most natives. The revision materials make clear, for example, that Britain did not stand entirely alone against the might of Nazi Germany during the period from June 1940 until June 1941, when Hitler invaded the Soviet Union. Britain's empire made a huge contribution to the war effort. India alone supplied nearly 1.5m troops, Canada sent 629,000, another 413,000 came from Australia, 128,500 from New Zealand, 136,000 from South African and 134,000 from other colonies.

Soldiers of all colours and religions put their lives on the line to support what Churchill described as the 'ancient motherland.' As well as supplying military muscle, the empire was a vital source of food for Britain throughout the war and also contributed money and weaponry on a vast scale. In short, had there been no empire to fall back on, Britain's resistance to Germany would have been severely weakened.

Another common misperception among British people concerns our contribution to defeating Germany. A YouGov poll in April 2018 asked respondents who they thought had played the most important role in defeating the Nazis during the Second World War. Half of those questioned said Britain, 13 per cent thought it was the Soviet Union, and nine per cent believed it was the United States. Given that Soviet forces killed nearly four out of five German soldiers who died in combat, and that the USSR suffered up to 31m war dead, half of them civilians, there is a very strong case to be made for the Soviet Union. The only other possible choice would be the USA. No historian or military expert would ever rank Britain in first place, yet despite the historical evidence to the contrary, one in two British people beg to differ.

But why does any of this matter? Put simply, because in a

democracy voters need to know their country's history, warts and all, in order to avoid being conned by patriotic myths and downright lies about the past. If, on the one hand we are constantly told we occupy the moral high ground because for six years we first resisted and then helped to defeat Fascism, while on the other we are deliberately kept in the dark about appalling abuses inflicted by our ancestors on weaker nations over four centuries, then inevitably we end up with a distorted national self-image. Ignorance of our past breeds both pride and prejudice, to coin a phrase, and this has far-reaching implications for our future.

Let's take the prejudice part first. Resentment of black and brown people living in Britain is based on the belief that they don't belong here. It's time for everyone to accept that the reason we have a multicultural society is because we had a multicultural empire, which in 1948 granted British citizenship to every single one of its inhabitants. The late Ambalavaner Sivanandan, Director of the Institute of Race Relations for 40 years, put it in a nutshell: 'We are here because you were there!'

Racism in the UK is a legacy that has outlasted even the government loan that was taken out to compensate the slave owners. The bill was finally paid off in 2015. But, two years later, Michael Boyle, whose family has been here since 1800, experienced the kind of routine racism that is commonplace for people of colour. He wrote in *The Guardian* about what happened to him soon after landing at Manchester airport on a flight from New York: 'At passport control I was asked where was I born. I replied, Liverpool, and joked: "Doesn't my accent give me away?" To which the officer replied, aggressively: "That's no guarantee you were born there." I'm a 73-year-old retired university lecturer, born and raised in Liverpool. But I'm black, you see, so my nationality always seems to be under question.'[7]

A more high-profile incident of this kind resulted in the resignation of Lady Susan Hussey, Queen Elizabeth's leading lady-in-waiting. At a high-profile royal event in 2022, Lady Susan reportedly interrogated Ngozi Fulani, the chief executive of a charity that helps victims of domestic violence, about where she was 'really from' and about her nationality. Like Michael Boyle, Ngozi Fulani is black and was born in Britain.

The same lack of historical perspective that fuels such everyday racism also underpins ill-informed comments by public figures. When Nigel Farage waded into the controversy surrounding Harry and Megan's interview with Oprah Winfrey, he made an astonishing claim when speaking on American television: 'I would put it to you that nobody in the world, in history, has done more for people of colour than the British royal family.'[8]

Distinguished black historian David Olusoga deftly demolished Farage's ludicrous remark in an article for *The*

Guardian: 'Even if he was referring only to the current monarch, this still represents something of a kick in the teeth for Nelson Mandela, Rosa Parks and Martin Luther King. If Farage meant the institution itself, this knowingly preposterous claim instantly crashes on the rocks of historical reality. Three British monarchs—Elizabeth I, Charles II and James II—were directly involved in the slave trade, and George III and William IV both defended slavery.'[9]

In January 2020, actor Laurence Fox claimed that by including a Sikh soldier in the Oscar-winning film *1917*, which is set in the First World War, the production was 'institutionally racist' and 'forcing diversity' on viewers. He said the Sikh's appearance in the film distracted from the plot.[10] As with Farage's gaffe, plenty of better-informed people came forward to teach Fox a history lesson. One of them was Sikh MP Tan Dhesi, who wrote in *The Daily Mirror*: 'I will take no lessons in patriotism or military service from a thespian blinkered by prejudice. My grandfather's brother, my grandmother's brother and another family member all fought voluntarily for Great Britain. One lost a leg. We know the price of freedom.'[11]

The film's director, Sam Mendes, was perhaps also at fault for only showing one solitary Sikh soldier, when in reality they served in regiments, not as individuals. More than 1.5m people from modern-day India, Pakistan, and Bangladesh, fought for Britain in the First World War. It was the same story in the Second World War. In Gravesend, Kent, there is a statue in honour of Squadron Leader Mahinder Singh Pujji DFC. He was a Sikh Hurricane pilot, who survived several crashes.

More serious than the occasional misguided public remark is institutional racism, where racist attitudes and remarks are tolerated in organisations as diverse as the Metropolitan Police and Yorkshire County Cricket Club. Following the murder of black teenager Stephen Lawrence in 1993, the Macpherson inquiry into how the police handled the investigation into his killing made 70 recommendations designed to demonstrate 'zero tolerance' for racism in society. They included measures to improve race relations and accountability not just in the police, but also in other public bodies including the civil service, the NHS and the judiciary.

Doreen Lawrence, Stephen's mother, is now a life peer in the House of Lords and one of many who believe that an essential step towards eradicating racism in the UK is to make teaching the history of empire compulsory: 'I hated history at school because it had nothing to do with me … I wanted the Macpherson report to ensure we opened up our lessons so kids in the class knew where they were from. If kids just hear that these people are over here taking our jobs, they will believe it. If they hear that in the past Britain has exploited every single aspect of the places these children come from, then perhaps they will see things differently.'[12]

For those who left school long ago, there are other routes to enlightenment. With 5m members, the National Trust, which looks after hundreds of stately homes and other historic properties, as well as large tracts of publicly accessible land, is one of the UK's best loved cultural institutions, second only to the BBC in the nation's affections. In 2020, it sparked a fierce debate when it published its *Interim Report on the Connections between Colonialism and Properties now in the Care of the National Trust, including Links with Historic Slavery.*

As Diane Roberts wrote in *Prospect* magazine, it represented: '115 pages of somewhat arid academic scholarship, listing 93 National Trust properties with links to trade in human beings and colonial injustices. Still, given the reaction in some quarters, you'd think they'd suggested turning Salisbury Cathedral into luxury flats or putting the Duchess of Sussex's face on the five pound note. The *Mail* harrumphed; *The Telegraph* seethed.' She went on to point out: 'Many white Britons still don't accept that black people have been part of their island story since at least the 1560s, when John Hawkins and Francis Drake got into the African slave trade.'[13]

Just like the Germans offended by Basil Fawlty's war allusions, mentioning profits from slavery and other ill-gotten gains invested in grand country piles now owned by the National Trust is seen by many British people as being in very poor taste, and by some as downright provocative. As

Diane Roberts adds in her *Prospect* article: 'The Trust set off a stink bomb at the fête by including Winston Churchill's country house Chartwell in its list of problematic properties, because Churchill was secretary of state for the colonies and, as prime minister during the war, exacerbated the 1943 Bengal famine, over the course of which 3m lives were lost.'

Similar outrage is expressed whenever there are suggestions that the British Museum should repatriate some of its treasures to their country of origin. The usual suspects in such debates are the *Elgin Marbles*, the classical Greek sculptures removed in the early 19th century from the *Parthenon* in Athens by the British Ambassador to the Ottoman court, Lord Elgin. They are the subject of a long-running dispute between Britain and Greece, as the latter would like to reclaim the treasures for a magnificent new archaeological museum at the foot of the *Acropolis*.

But at least the *Marbles* were acquired in exchange for money. There are two other cultural works in the British Museum's collection that are even more controversial because they were seized in violent circumstances. The *Maqdala* treasures were plundered in 1868 after 13,000 British troops ransacked the imperial palace complex in Abyssinia as part of an operation to free a handful of British hostages. A British Museum curator was there to oversee the plunder, which required 15 elephants and 200 mules to transport. The other infamous collection of military spoils is the *Benin Bronzes*. These were seized when the British sent 1,400 armed men to take control of the Niger Delta in 1897. Tens of thousands of Edo people died in the assault, which also saw thousands of works in bronze and ivory removed from the Benin palace before it was burnt to the ground. Some 900 of these looted works are now housed at the British Museum. Despite these well documented sackings, there would appear to be a distinct lack of empathy on the part of museum curators in the UK. As *Empireland* author Sathnam Sanghera puts it: 'Imagine how the British would feel if the French had won the Napoleonic wars, occupied Britain and transferred Stonehenge to Lille.'[14]

In fact, the French are showing more looter's remorse than their cross-channel neighbours. In 2017, President Macron pledged that France would return any items his country had taken from Africa. Three years later, the French Senate approved the return of 27 pieces of African heritage from the country's national collections to their original locations in Benin and the Ivory Coast. Elsewhere in Europe, the Netherlands, Germany and Belgium have all established commissions and issued reports on colonial collections in their national museums. The priority is to return objects which have blood on them.

In December 2022, the German foreign minister Annalena Baerbock symbolically handed 21 *Benin Bronzes* back to Nigeria (they had been sold by Britain to German museums).

At the handover ceremony, Nigeria's culture minister Lai Mohammed regretted the lack of similar cooperation from the main British repository for *Benin Bronzes*: 'I met a brick wall', he said. 'The British Museum must understand that repatriation is a turn whose time has come.'

In 2019 Rehana Watkinson (@Rehune) from Birmingham used her Twitter account to poke fun at the hypocrisy inherent in British justifications for holding onto foreign cultural objects: 'How come some people have no problem telling some people to "go back home" but ask them to repatriate one little thing from the British Museum and it's all, "This precious inanimate object from someone else's culture BELONGS HERE?"'

On the morning of Thursday 9 January 2020, something unusual happened on the London Underground. It wasn't that the trains were all running on time. Instead, a group of sixth form students from South London, all with family links to former British colonies, distributed 5,000 fake copies of the free *Metro* newspaper to commuters at 20 tube stations across the capital. 'Boris backs empire education' ran its headline. This is of course not yet the case, or at least not in the way the students who organised the stunt intended. Because although empire history is available as an option for pupils aged 11 to 14 (key stage three), it is not compulsory. The same goes for the slave trade. The campaign, *Fill in the*

Blanks, wants empire teaching to be made mandatory for all key stage three students.

In the article they wrote for the fake edition of the '*Metro*', the students put the following words into the mouth of the then prime minister: 'As Britain forms its post-Brexit identity, the Conservative party recognises the importance of providing a balanced assessment of the British Empire, colonisation and slavery. In order to avoid replicating our past mistakes, this new era of national sovereignty must be built on a realistic appraisal of our history. Colonialism, migration and empire are central themes of our national story and, from today, the telling will no longer be incomplete.'

These elegantly expressed thoughts are still waiting to be uttered by an occupant of 10 Downing Street. But the article did contain some authentic quotes. One was from Dr Andrea Major, a professor of British colonial history at the University of Leeds: 'We need better education and more open public debate on all aspects of British colonial history, warts and all. This is needed to successfully combat our collective amnesia about the levels of violence, exploitation and racism involved in many aspects of imperialism.'[15]

Britain is of course by no means the only European country whose empire inflicted suffering on many peoples across the world. The Dutch, the French, the Spanish, and the Belgians all have unpleasant and repressive colonial histories.

What sets Britain apart is its imperial nostalgia, based on ignorance—and therefore unencumbered by any sense of contrition.

One phrase which recent Conservative prime ministers have been fond of using is, 'Global Britain.' If, indeed, we are to seek our post-Brexit trading fortunes in distant countries, then we ought to recognise that Global Britain has a global history. If an appeal to morality and common decency cannot sway the argument for compulsory colonial history teaching, then self-interest should surely do the trick. Before we launch into our sales pitch to a potential foreign customer, we should at least know how well we treated their country when it was under British rule.

But we need to go much further, and many people will have to play their part. Television producers should make fewer documentaries about romantic journeys on railways built by the British in India, and more films about the subcontinent's fabled textile industry, which was deliberately destroyed by our colonial ancestors. Museum directors should examine both their consciences and their extensive collections and return stolen cultural artefacts to their rightful owners. Most of all, our leaders need to make formal apologies for the atrocities we committed on colonial soil. Somebody needs to go to Kenya, to India, and yes, to China, to say sorry for what we did. Just make sure it isn't Basil Fawlty.

CHAPTER 8

A 93 PER CENT SOLUTION TO A SEVEN PER CENT PROBLEM

Pruning private school privilege

In 1974, the American author Nicholas Meyer wrote a pastiche Sherlock Holmes novel, in which the famous London detective created by Sir Arthur Conan Doyle attempts to kick his cocaine habit by travelling to Vienna to meet the equally renowned psychoanalyst, Sigmund Freud. A key factor in the detective's recovery is a kidnapping mystery, which of course he eventually solves, thereby saving Europe from an all-engulfing war. Meyer called his book *The Seven Per Cent Solution.*

Unlike Sherlock Holmes, the UK has a seven per cent problem. That's the percentage of children who attend fee-paying schools, compared with the 93 per cent taught within the state sector. It's problematic because a private school education confers such huge social and economic advantages that it leads to a monoculture of political leadership and a stranglehold on the country's centres of power, influence and affluence. Stark statistics speak for themselves. The independent school sector accounts for a staggering 74 per cent of senior judges, 71 per cent of senior officers in the armed services, 55 per cent of top civil servants in Whitehall and 50 per cent of Cabinet ministers and members of the House of Lords. More than four out of ten newspaper columnists were privately educated, and so too were four out of five of the main presenters of BBC Radio 4's prestigious *Today* programme. Amol Rajan is the sole state school alumnus.

The benefits of a private education extend to the worlds of sport and entertainment. In 2012 and 2016, half of the British Olympic team were independent school alumni. The same goes for 60 per cent of recent British Oscar winners and 42 per cent of BAFTA winners. Tom Hiddleston, Dominic West, Damian Lewis and Eddie Redmayne all went to Eton. Benedict Cumberbatch was at Harrow. It's a far cry from the 1960s when working-class actors like Richard Burton, Sean Connery and Michael Caine dominated the silver screen.

A survey in 2010 found that 60 per cent of artists in the pop music charts attended private school, compared with just one per cent two decades earlier.[1] The list includes

James Blunt, Chris Martin, Mumford & Sons, La Roux, Florence Welch, Pixie Lott, Lily Allen, Eliza Doolittle and Mark Ronson. As TV presenter and author Stewart Maconie laments in his book, *The Nanny State Made Me*, 'Where have all the Erics, Joes, Bills, Georges and Brians gone, that formed the rock elite of the 1960s and 70s? Top indie act The Maccabees included a Hugo, an Orlando, a Felix and a Rupert.'[2]

But the area in which the seven per cent problem is most consequential is national leadership. Boris Johnson was the 20th Old Etonian to enter Downing Street, closely following in the footsteps of his distant relation, David Cameron. For more than 200 years, there have only been four elected British prime ministers who were not privately educated: Harold Wilson, Edward Heath, Margaret Thatcher and John Major all went to grammars. Liz Truss, Gordon Brown and James Callaghan, who all entered Number 10 without winning a general election, are the only premiers who went to non-selective state schools. Liz Truss appointed a cabinet that was lauded for its gender and ethnic diversity, but 59 per cent of her ministers attended independent schools whose fees are far beyond the reach of ordinary families.

Many Labour leaders, including Clement Attlee, Michael Foot and Tony Blair, also attended private schools. Jeremy Corbyn went to a prep school in Shropshire, while his chief of staff, Seamus Milne (son of a former BBC Director General) went to Winchester College, one of the country's top public schools and the same alma mater as Rishi Sunak.

Even the Liberal-Democrats prefer privately educated leaders, including current incumbent Ed Davey, who attended the fee-paying Nottingham High, and his predecessor Nick Clegg, an alumnus of the exclusive Westminster School.

In 1990 a different Nick began offering group therapy to what he called 'boarding school survivors.' He later wrote a book called *Wounded Leaders,* based on his experiences with the young men who attended his sessions. One of Nick Duffell's main conclusions was that public schools are not a good preparation for pupils who go on to wield political power. 'British elitism supports an outdated leadership style that is unable to rise above its own interests, perceive the bigger picture and go beyond a familiar, entrenched and unhealthy system of adversarial politics. Such a leadership style is not to be recommended. It may well be dangerous, given the demands of the modern world in which problems are increasingly communal, indeed global, and in which solutions urgently demand non-polarised cooperation and a clear focus on the common good in order to take effect on a worldwide scale.'[3]

This is a view endorsed by Professor Diane Reay of Cambridge University, author of *Miseducation.* A former state schoolteacher from a working-class background, she warns of the dangers of elite leaders deprived of contact during their school years with working-class contemporaries. 'They are making decisions for the rest of us based on a very, very slim knowledge base about what the rest of us are like, what our attitudes and values are, what our needs are, and how we live our lives. That is deeply problematic, because where you have people who have been segregated from the rest of the community, there clearly is a lack of empathy and understanding.'[4]

In his book, *Posh Boys—How English Public Schools Ruin Britain*, journalist Robert Verkaik describes how our system of educational apartheid works: 'Imagine a world where leaders are able to directly pass power to their children. These children are plucked from their nurseries and sent to beautiful compounds far away from all the other children. They are provided with all the teachers they need, the best facilities, doctors and food. They are introduced to the greatest thinkers and allowed to see and touch the finest art. Each day they are told this is because they are the brightest and most important children in the world. Later, in the outside world, they are presented with the best jobs, the grandest houses and most of the money. Through their network of friends and family, they control the government, the army, the police and the City. The leaders tell all of their people that everyone is equal and that everyone has the chance to become a leader, but this isn't true, because the leaders have made it impossible for the other people's children to become leaders.'[5]

Novelist Tony Parsons, himself a product of a grammar school education, is more blunt in his description of the UK's two-tier system: 'It has become a commonplace to say that we are now living in a post-meritocracy, where it is not what you can do that counts, but how much money your parents blew on your education … Such is the depth of our educational apartheid that a thick rich kid will now always do better than a bright poor kid. And that should break our hearts.'[6]

So how does the system work in practice? In today's Britain, the passport to the best-paid jobs is a degree from Oxbridge or a top Russell Group university such as Warwick, University College London (UCL) or the London School of Economics (LSE). To be admitted to such universities, you need top exam grades at GCSE and A-level and a convincingly written personal statement. Because private schools have significantly greater teaching resources than their state-funded counterparts, they are relentlessly efficient exam factories that churn out consistently excellent results.

Writing in *The Guardian*, Frances Ryan exposed the wide gap in academic outcomes. 'In the year before the pandemic, the Sutton Trust found independent school pupils were seven times as likely to gain a place at Oxbridge than those in non-selective state schools, and more than twice as likely to take a place at Russell Group institutions. In 2018 another study found nearly half of 'clever but disadvantaged' students failed to secure top GCSE grades. Just 52 per cent of the disadvantaged high achievers at primary school gained at least five A*- and A-grades in England, compared with 72 per cent of their wealthier, equally clever, peers.'[7]

Interestingly however, studies have shown that, on average, privately educated students end up with lower class degrees than state counterparts with similar A-level results. One explanation is that the latter achieve lower A-level grades than they would have obtained had they had the same level of support as private school pupils. At university, where autonomous study is the name of the game, there is, for the first time since nursery school, a level academic playing field that allows habitually self-reliant state pupils to fulfil their academic potential.

But while the class of university degree might be obtained under more equal conditions, the same is not true when it comes to getting offers for internships. These holiday work experience stints are as vital as academic qualifications for building the glittering CV that will land you a well-paid job after graduation. It's much easier to get an internship at an investment bank or a magic circle law firm if your school friends' parents work for the likes of Goldman Sachs or Clifford Chance. It may indeed be just a question of informally asking around to see whose Mum or Dad can pull a few strings to get you a two-month summer internship. So much the better if your own parents also have high-powered jobs in desirable professions. This gives you a potential bargaining chip. Of course, if you go to a state school in a deprived area, your single mum is a cleaner and your mates' parents drive buses or work at the Tesco checkout, then your internship options are somewhat more limited.

Even if a working-class student succeeds in getting an interview for a job or a placement, they're at a big disadvantage compared with privately educated candidates. A study by the Social Mobility Commission found that City firms place as much importance on a person's speech, accent, dress and behaviour as their skills and qualifications. It gave the example of banks whose corporate finance divisions regard wearing brown shoes together with a business suit as unacceptable behaviour.[8] One employer frankly admitted his firm's recruitment practices were loaded against young working-class applicants. But, he asked, 'How much mud do I have to sift through in that population to find a diamond?'

One under-privileged candidate said he was told after being rejected at interview: 'You're not quite the fit for this bank. You're not polished enough.' Acquiring the necessary social skills—succinctly formulated as 'polish and push'—is an integral part of an expensive school education, as evidenced by the number of their alumni who work for the most prestigious financial institutions. At least 34 per cent of newly recruited investment bankers went to a fee-paying school, despite that sector representing just seven per cent of the total number of UK school children.

The then head of the Social Mobility Commission, Alan Milburn, complained that 'Bright working-class kids are being systematically locked out of top jobs in investment banking because they may not attend a small number of elite universities or understand arcane culture rules.'[9] Joanne Moore, from the ARC Network, who led research into life sciences, confirmed it was the same story in her sector: 'In life sciences, graduate jobs often focus on a candidate's practical skills as well as academic criteria—which may be more limited for non-privileged students who face barriers to taking up placements and internships.'[10]

Even in employment, academic origins continue to exert their influence. A 2021 study by the Social Mobility Commission, this time in cooperation with the LSE, involved a survey of more than 300,000 civil servants.[11] It found that those from poorer backgrounds were much less likely to climb what one described as 'the velvet drainpipe' to the top, with the vast majority of senior roles occupied by people from privileged backgrounds. Overall, only 18 per cent of the 6,000 highest graded staff came from disadvantaged homes, while one in four had been to independent schools. Among the elite mandarins (permanent secretaries, like Sir

Humphrey in *Yes Prime Minister),* this proportion rose to six out of 10. To be successful, ambitious bureaucrats have to master a behavioural code known as 'studied neutrality' which involves speaking in a cut-glass Received Pronunciation (RP) accent and casually dropping Latin phrases into conversations.

Just like the gender pay gap, there's an education pay gap, and it's getting wider. In 1991, privately educated 33 to 34-year-olds were earning on average 25 per cent more than their similarly qualified state-educated counterparts. By 2004, the private school pay premium had risen to 41 per cent. Remember, too, that the vast majority of privately educated children have their university tuition fees and living costs fully paid by their parents or grandparents. After all, if a family can afford to pay school fees, it can easily afford to pay the much cheaper fees charged by universities. It's mostly state school educated children who are burdened with paying off their student loans once they get a job paying more than £22,000 a year.

So, for several reasons, it literally pays to go to an independent, fee-paying school. But how do these noble institutions, which are officially registered as charities, work their magic? You don't need to be Sherlock Holmes to solve this mystery. When schools are charging fees up to five times as much as universities, you're bound to get some return on your money.

Millfield has an equestrian centre, clay pigeon shooting,

two recording studios and a 350-seat concert hall. Stowe has a golf course and its own school nightclub. More than 800 private schools have tennis courts, 633 have Astroturf pitches and 595 have swimming pools. According to former England cricketer and commentator Ed Smith, the smoothest outfield he ever played on was at Lords, the home of world cricket. The second best was at his private school in Tonbridge. And if you were wondering why there are so many toffs among the luvvies currently treading the boards, the answer may lie in a 2017 *Sunday Times* investigation that found that private schools in London and the home counties have 59 theatres, many of them state-of-the-art, compared with the 42, often shabby, stages located in the capital's West End.[12]

One of the most popular West End musicals of all time was *Oliver!*, based on the Dickens novel, *Oliver Twist*. Among its hit songs was *Food, Glorious Food*, which deploys lashings of irony to deplore the lack of quality sustenance on offer at Mr Bumble's workhouse. The starving boys in that miserable establishment would have been shocked had they been able to visit the refectories of today's private schools. At St Paul's Girls School in London, for example, a typical menu features such sophisticated fare as Spanish smoky samfaina with eggs and rocket, slow-baked Moroccan lamb with broad beans, prunes and preserved lemon and Malaysian snapper curry with okra and tomato.

During the pandemic, it was revealed that children in private and state schools were receiving very different school meal packages from two branches of the same catering business. While Chartwells UK regaled poorer kids with tins of beans, packets of pasta and sundry fruit and veg, its sister company, Chartwells Independent, was posting mouth-watering photos on Instagram of its selection of canapés, bouillabaisse and salmon wrapped in coconut, lemongrass and banana leaf. These delicacies were of course destined for private schools.

It's a similar story of privilege when it comes to accommodation. 'Chic interiors, designer lighting, ocean views and a rave review in *Tatler*' is *The Daily Telegraph's* description of accommodation at the exclusive Roedean School for girls in Sussex.[13] Comfy en-suite rooms equipped with the latest high-speed internet connections are now standard issue for boarders. No wonder that journalist Ben Chu joked that Britain's private schools are 'luxury country clubs with quite a nice school attached.' In a similar spirit, left-wing playwright David Hare, himself a product of Lancing private school, quipped that: 'Private schools have changed from places where you are flogged, to places you flog.'[14]

But putting the jokes and the frills to one side, the real benefit of a private education is the lower pupil/teacher ratio. In 2016 this stood at 8.6:1 in fee-paying schools, compared with 17:1 in the state sector. This represents a huge advantage, as Francis Green and David Kynaston explain in their book, *Engines of Privilege—Britain's Private School Problem*: 'While teachers in the private sector are less likely to have a teaching qualification, proportionately more private school teachers obtained degrees from high-ranking universities and earned good grades; more also have a post-graduate qualification, and more are specialists in maths and sciences, typically the subjects where teachers are in short supply.'[15]

Indeed, shortages in the state sector are aggravated by the poaching of some of their best teachers by private schools. In 2017-18, nearly 2,000 experienced teachers at state schools left to join the private sector.

Writing in *The New European*, education campaigner Fiona Millar explains how the superior financial resources of independent schools also provide 'the chance to layer ever more opportunities, enrichment and confidence on the already privileged. Whether it is through intensive university preparation, outlandish uniforms, networks, the use of absurd language like spaffing or girly swot, or the sense that they are grooming leaders, the system is designed to ensure that pupils emerge feeling better than, and different from, everyone else.'[16]

Some have described the huge investment by private schools in teaching staff and infrastructure that started in the 1980s as an educational arms race and of course such races never come cheap. In real terms, school fees have tripled since the 1980s, leaving many middle-class parents struggling to keep up. Indeed, today's fees have reached such eye watering levels that perhaps the most appropriate song from the repertoire of *Oliver!* is the gang leader Fagin's melodious tutorial in light-fingered petty crime: *You've Got To Pick a Pocket or Two*. And you need deep pockets indeed to pay for even a modest private school education.

A study carried out in 2021 by the website PoundToy found that the most expensive boarding school in the country was Cherwell College in Oxford, where the annual fee was £58,500.[17] Counter-intuitively, two of the country's most prestigious establishments, Eton College and Harrow School, charged considerably less at £42,501 and £42,600 respectively. Another surprising finding was that the most expensive day school, the Oracle in Congleton, Cheshire, was much dearer than even the priciest boarding school, with sky high annual fees of £96,816 per child (at those rates it would have probably been cheaper to have been taught in Ancient Greece by the original Oracle at Delphi).

Of the most expensive boarding schools, 29 of the top 30 are located in southern England. The only exception is the modestly named Cardiff Sixth Form College. At £46,449 a year, there's nothing modest about its annual fees, which explain its 11th place in the table. The study also lists the country's 50 most affordable independent schools.

Only the top (i.e., cheapest) three have fees lower than

what it costs to attend a UK university. And 28 out of the 50 charge more than £20,000 a year for boarders, which would still present a huge financial strain for anyone earning the 2020 median UK salary of £31,141. With two children at such 'affordable' establishments, the study estimated their family income would have to exceed £120,000 in order to meet the school bills with relative ease.

With fees like this, it should come as no surprise that the number of teachers at private schools who earn over £100,000 a year has leapt by 25 per cent in just two years. In this league table, compiled by *The Sunday Times*, Eton College is in pole position, with 47 staff earning a six-figure sum.[18] Harrow had 16 staff and Brighton College 12 in this top bracket.

Some head teachers are paid more than £300,000 a year, arguing that they are running global businesses with schools in China, Central Asia and the Middle East. Whether they deserve to earn significantly more than the British prime minister or the CEO of NHS England is debatable. What is beyond doubt is that they are among the world's best-paid charity workers (most private schools are registered as charities). In their case, charity clearly does begin at home.

For many of these top earners, 'home' is in one of the nine so-called Clarendon Schools, which form the Premier League of the country's 2,600 independent schools. Charterhouse, Eton, Harrow, Merchant Taylor's, Rugby,

Shrewsbury, St Paul's, Westminster and Winchester may not charge the highest fees or obtain the best exam results, but they are nevertheless regarded as the gold standard of independent education, thanks to a centuries-old track record of successfully propelling their alumni into the commanding heights of the British Establishment. According to a recent study by two academics from the London School of Economics, Clarendon pupils are 94 times more likely to reach the top elite positions in society than anyone who attended other schools.[19]

Despite educating just 0.15 per cent of the population (that's fewer than one in every 500 pupils), these private institutions still produce nearly 10 per cent of entrants on the prestigious *Who's Who* biographical list, a directory which includes MPs, peers, senior civil servants, judges and museum directors. Of the 54 prime ministers elected to office in Great Britain, a staggering 36 (or 67 per cent) were educated at a Clarendon school. Even among students who attended Oxbridge, alumni from the Clarendon Schools are around twice as likely to reach the elite as non-Clarendon educated Oxbridge graduates.

Dr Aaron Reeves and Dr Sam Friedman from LSE speculated on the reasons for the Clarendon Schools' extraordinary success in supplying so many of the country's movers and shakers. 'Clearly their power lies beyond simple academic excellence and may be rooted in an extensive extra-curricular education—particularly in terms of sport, culture and taste—that endows old boys and girls with a particular way of being in the world that signals elite male status to others.'[20]

Sometimes, this elite male status signalling can take extremely distasteful forms. The Oxford students who belong to the notorious Bullingdon and Piers Gaveston clubs share three things in common: they are male, wealthy and educated at a premier league private school, most commonly Eton. Their rituals are well documented and include smashing-up restaurants and running riot through the streets of Oxford. It is said that a prospective Bullingdon club member has to burn a £50 note in front of a homeless person. Piers Gaveston has an even more unsavoury reputation—in one well-publicised case it is rumoured to have found innovative uses for the head of a dead pig.

Given their current reputation for boorish behaviour, it will no doubt come as a surprise to some readers to discover that the male pupils of the original public schools were (almost literally) choir boys in comparison with their modern-day counterparts. This is because the first such schools were set up to cater for boys from the poorest local families, in the true tradition of Christian charity. Indeed, the very first school—Winchester—was set up in 1382 by William of Wykeham, Bishop of Winchester and a trusted royal counsellor. The new school was intended as a feeder school for

New College, Oxford, which William founded three years earlier to teach theology, law and the arts.

The aim of the first public schools was therefore to provide an ecclesiastical education for the children of the poor. At the outset, Winchester had 70 free scholars, corresponding to the number of disciples sent by Jesus to spread the Gospel of St Luke. St Paul's, founded in 1509, had 153 pupils, matching the number of species of fish believed to exist in the world, according to St John's Gospel. The charter of Merchant Taylor's School, established in 1561, stated that it should cater for 250 pupils, of whom 100 must be 'poor men's sons.' The fees for the other 150 were modest.

By the early 19th century, however, the noble principles of the founders had already been undermined by their greedy successors. At Winchester, the free scholars had become a small minority. When the school's governors were asked to account for the preponderance of rich pupils at a school set up to benefit the poor, they disingenuously replied that all the pupils were very poor because 'it is only their parents who were rich' (the public schools have since developed more sophisticated arguments to justify their elitist social composition). By 1861, of the 2,283 boys attending Eton, Winchester, Westminster, Harrow, Rugby, Shrewsbury and Charterhouse, all but 342 were fee payers.

As *Posh Boys* author Robert Verkaik observes, 'Wykeham's educational ideal had been usurped by England's rich and powerful families. The word "public" had taken on a whole new meaning, so that schools opened their doors to all the nation's wealthy families, no matter where they lived or what religion they practised. The public schools were founded to educate the poor and ended up serving the interests of the rich.'[21]

But, while they may have served the interests of the rich, the public schools of the 18th and 19th centuries did very little to serve the interests of the country. The inventors of the spinning jenny, water frame, steam engine and many other innovations that powered the Industrial Revolution were mainly from humble backgrounds and went to modest schools. Britain's most celebrated engineer, Isambard Kingdom Brunel, was initially taught at home by his father, himself a famous engineer, before being educated in France.

Indeed, their obsession with Greek and Latin meant that the public schools were a handicap for pupils with a scientific bent. Charles Darwin said of Shrewsbury school: 'Nothing could have been worse for the development of my mind than Dr Butler's school, as it was strictly classical, nothing else being taught except a little ancient geography and history. The school as a means of education was simply a blank.'[22]

Despite producing more soldiers than scientists, claims that the public schools were behind Britain's military successes against Napoleon are exaggerated. The Duke of Wellington, although born and bred in Ireland, did indeed attend Eton College for three years. His loneliness there led him to hate the school, and it is therefore highly unlikely that he really said, 'The Battle of Waterloo was won on the playing fields of Eton.' All the more so because Eton had no playing fields at the time he was there.

But, while fee paying schools may not be able to claim any credit for military battles in the early 19th century, they can award themselves distinguished service medals for winning a series of political battles in the second half of the 20th, when they succeeded brilliantly in defeating education reformers who wanted to dilute their social elitism and remove their charitable status.

As hinted at earlier, the country's leading public schools are a strange kind of charity. For one thing, they are run like big businesses. Eton College received more than £42m in school fees in 2020. It has nearly a thousand staff, of whom nearly 200 are teachers. Its headmaster is paid on the same scale as a FTSE 100 chief executive. The school also has seven subsidiary businesses, focusing on hospitality, commercial education and property development. In addition to annual income, Eton has endowment funds, securities and investment property portfolios worth nearly £500m. By way of comparison, the late Queen Elizabeth's Duchy of Lancaster Estate, from which she drew an income, was valued at £472m in 2015.

The Eton estates include nearly 400 buildings and historic colleges, many of them located in the town which shares its name. The school owns 175,000 works of art and antiques, including a collection of Egyptian antiquities bequeathed by a former pupil. Many of the artefacts are priceless.

But one thing Eton does not have is overseas branches. Harrow started the globe-trotting trend by setting up in Bangkok. In the intervening two decades, more than 70 independent schools have followed suit by establishing at least one sister school abroad, or a partnership with an international school. They include Dulwich College, Rugby, Marlborough College, Wellington College, Wycombe Abbey, Shrewsbury, Repton, Malvern College, Merchiston Castle, Haileybury and Sherborne. Harrow now has five sister schools and Dulwich College 10. China, Central Asia and the Middle East are favourite regions for expansion.

Trading on the brand reputation of their British alma mater, these foreign business ventures are a nice little earner. But they have been severely condemned by some politicians. In a speech to the House of Lords in 2017, Andrew Adonis expressed his outrage at an ambitious commercial venture by one of the country's top rated public schools: 'Only yesterday Westminster School, a wholly owned charitable subsidiary of the Church of England, which occupies fabulous premises adjoining Westminster Abbey, announced that it was setting up six elite schools in China. Its social outreach should be to the poor of Bradford, not the super-rich of Beijing!'[23]

There are not many businesses with extensive overseas operations that can claim charitable status. For the 52 per cent of private schools who do, there are big financial benefits. It entitles them to an 80 per cent discount on business rates (state schools must pay the full cost). For Eton, this represented a saving of £4.1m from 2017-22. VAT exemption is another perk of charitable status, meaning, among other things, that school fees are 20 per cent lower than they would be otherwise.

An unlikely opponent of both concessions was Michael Gove, who was coruscating in an article that appeared in *The Times* in 2017: 'There is one group of highly successful enterprises that is pretty much insulated from the present row about business rates. Our private schools. Because charities get an 80 per cent exemption from the levy. And, to my continuing surprise, we still consider the education of the children of plutocrats and oligarchs to be a charitable activity'. He further argued that VAT exemption on school fees 'allows the wealthiest in this country, indeed the very wealthiest in the globe, to buy a prestige service that secures their children a permanent positional edge in society at an effective 20 per cent discount.'[24]

To justify their charitable status, the independent schools have to provide data to prove to the Charity Commission that they contribute to the public benefit. Desperate examples include the existence of public rights of way across school land, school open days and pupils taking part in village fetes. But it has to be said that there are also some more convincing charitable initiatives. Some private schools have for years been making genuine efforts to open their doors to children from working- and middle-class families with modest means.

Christ's Hospital, near Horsham in Sussex, is a prime example. Thanks to its large endowments, it has succeeded in substantially honouring the wishes of its 16th century founders that it should seek to provide a boarding school education for children from poorer families. It helps 75 per cent of its pupils with means-tested bursaries ranging from a 100 per cent to a five per cent fees discount.

Another laudable initiative came from Wellington College, which invested £2m in setting up the Wellington Academy, a state school in Tidworth, Wiltshire. In 2020, Eton College announced plans to offer 100 per cent bursaries for 140 boys by 2025, representing 10 per cent of the total, and to make available its range of online self-learning courses to all state schools, free of charge.

No one denies that disadvantaged children who are offered a *Willy Wonka*-style golden ticket for free education in a private school can reap huge personal benefits. Writing in *Prospect* magazine, Kiran Samrai recounted her own positive experiences as a scholarship girl, while also acknowledging the unfairness of a system that fails so many children from similarly poor backgrounds:

'I am an East London girl, state-educated for most of my life. I was born in a council flat, raised by a single mother, as close to a Jeremy Kyle byline that the voyeuristic liberal gaze requires me to be. In Year Nine of secondary school, I won a full scholarship to a private school. The classes were small, the teachers were not overworked or underpaid; when a student was troubled, they noticed, and they had the resources to intervene. I got the pastoral and emotional support I needed—they even paid for me to go to therapy. These are the invisible support networks that elite educational spaces are able to provide to a select few, and that comprehensives, increasingly, can no longer afford to. It's no wonder that the privately educated elite continue to dominate top jobs in almost every field.'[25]

Full scholarships like the one awarded to Kiran Samrai are extremely rare. Using data provided by the Charity Commission, a study published in 2021 by academics from Welsh, Finnish and Australian universities found that, during the 2018-19 school year, only one per cent of all private school students received a full scholarship. According to one of the researchers, Dr Malcom James: 'Given the level of fees, the overwhelming majority of scholarship students still require very substantial family contributions.

Many scholarships may, in practice, be awarded to middle or upper-class families. Scholarships may therefore do little to make schools genuinely more socially inclusive.'[26]

Worse still, the researchers found that many schools exaggerated the costs of scholarships in their financial accounts, thereby allowing the schools to appear to provide more public benefit than they really do. The report called it: 'Virtue signalling their generosity.' This finding is alarming because fee discounts are the main way in which most private schools seek to justify their charitable status.

According to an investigation by *The Byline Times* newspaper, during the six years from 2016 to 2022, the Clarendon schools grew their assets by £600m, or 44 per cent.[27] Compare this with a nine per cent cut in state secondary school per pupil spending during the decade from 2010 to 2020.

Private education is an awkward subject to broach for a number of reasons. In my own case, some of my best friends went to private school and have sent their own children there. My sister was a teacher in the private sector, and both she and my brother sent their children to private schools. Because education is such a key determinant of future success in the jobs market, many parents feel conflicted between their political principles and their family responsibilities.

This ambivalence—let's call it normative dissonance—was neatly summed up by the Dutch journalist, Joris Luyendijk, who wrote in *Prospect* magazine that: 'It is quite ironic that a nation that gave the world the term "fair play" sees the fact that rich children receive a better education than poor ones as a perfectly natural thing. I remember asking around at *The Guardian*, where I had been hired to investigate the City of London, why this progressive newspaper did not put the school system centre stage. The answer: most of our management and prominent writers went to private school themselves and most are sending their children there too, so that would invite the charge of hypocrisy.'[28]

Television presenter and media commentator Mehdi Hasan, who was himself privately educated, agrees that the subject is deliberately avoided by journalists and politicians alike: 'It's one of the biggest taboos in British politics; the educational elephant in the room. Too many politicians and pundits would much rather argue about the challenge of grade inflation, the future of gold-plated A-levels or the role of the teaching unions than address the reality: that the great rift in our education system is between our best schools, most of which are private, and the schools ordinary families rely on. Shamefully, the rest of us also turn a blind eye to this grotesque educational apartheid in our midst.'[29]

Playwright and grammar schoolboy Alan Bennett explained his opposition to fee-paying schools during an address in 2014 at Kings College Chapel in Cambridge. 'My objection to private education is simply put. It is not fair. And to say that nothing is fair is not an answer. Governments, even this one, exist to make the nation's circumstances more fair, but no parliament, whatever its complexion, has dared to tackle private education.'[30]

But some leading figures in politics and the media are prepared to publicly call out the inherent unfairness of our two-tier education system. Michael Gove was education secretary from 2010-14. Three years later, he wrote a caustic article in *The Times:* 'Are the children of the rich intrinsically more talented and worthy, more gifted and more deserving of celebration than the rest? Of course not. But our state-subsidised private schools continue to give them every possible advantage. Private schools have facilities, and provide opportunities, that most state school students could scarcely envisage and which most five-star hotels would struggle to provide. The fees for these schools are all more than £30,000 per year, per pupil, well above the average annual salary of most Britons. They are out of reach for all but the very wealthiest, or most fortunate. And yet they are all registered charities with huge tax exemptions. How many students from Knowsley, Sunderland, Merthyr Tydfil or Blyth Valley ever cross the thresholds of private schools?'[31]

Author, journalist, disc jockey and self-styled 'professional northerner,' Stewart Maconie, is even more brutal in his analysis of what should be done to address the UK's seven per cent problem: 'Let's be absolutely straight about this. Any opinion other than the conviction that private education should be abolished immediately is cant and bullshit. It may be tough. It may mean your kids have to work harder to get on. It may make your domestic life less smooth. But so did abolishing slavery for the comfortably off. Privilege and unfairness will never be eradicated; social justice will never be achieved while well-meaning but hand-wringing liberals pay to send their children to private schools. Sorry guys, but it's hypocrisy, and you know it. Abolish them. Turn them into Aldis, sports halls and nail bars. Today.'[32]

But why should we care if people with plenty of money spend it on their children's education? Surely it's a personal choice, like buying a Porsche, flying business class or paying for a private health plan? Freedom of choice for consumers is a key pillar of liberal democracies and is not usually subject to state interference. But the reason why education cannot be compared with other consumer goods and services is that the outcomes it produces are qualitatively different. Whether we drive a Mercedes or a Skoda, we all get from A to B. Whether we fly business or economy, we all arrive at the same airport. Whether we have private health insurance or rely on the NHS, we all eventually receive the same quality of healthcare from the same doctors.

But, when it comes to education, the choice between private and state leads to very different socio-economic destinations. To return to the aviation analogy, we're not just travelling in different sections of the same plane, we're on different planes going to different airports. Those who pay for private education are paying to improve their child's life chances, and since the number of places at top universities and well-paying jobs are limited, this comes at the expense of children whose parents cannot afford to do the same. It is therefore impossible to simultaneously believe in the right to private education and the existence of equality of opportunity.

Defenders of private education often argue that they are paying twice for their children's education, once through income and council taxes that go towards maintaining the state schools that they choose not to use, and secondly through the school fees levied by their preferred private sector supplier. This line of argument was given short shrift by the Newsom Committee, which in 1968 made recommendations for reforming private education. 'Every taxpayer and ratepayer contributes towards public services, whether or not he or she uses them. Fee-paying parents are therefore no different from single people or married couples without children.'[33] *Times* columnist and former Tory MP Matthew Parris put it more bluntly: 'I dismiss out of hand the hoary old argument that private schools save taxpayers the cost of educating pupils in state schools. You might as well claim charitable status for your car on the ground that it saves local authorities the cost of subsidising your seat on the bus.'[34]

As well as poaching thousands of state-trained teachers

each year and receiving substantial financial subsidies thanks to their charitable status, private schools also deprive the state sector of the kind of pushy middle-class parents who would mercilessly hound their local and national politicians to improve the quality of comprehensive schooling, if that was the only academic option available to them. The Newsom Committee put it more succinctly: 'If all influential parents had children in maintained schools they would have brought pressure on Parliament and Whitehall to make them better than they are.'[35]

In their book *Engines of Privilege*, Francis Green and David Kynaston highlight the resources imbalance that continues to favour private schools: 'Most provide a high quality academic and broad education for those who attend them. However, looked at from the perspective of the whole country's education system, the concentration of so many resources on one small, privileged sector is hugely wasteful: the people who work in private schools and the extensive facilities could do so much more for the nation's children if they were spread around more evenly among those children.'[36]

As things stand, Britain spends more on private education than any other country in the developed world: £9bn in school fees plus £760m from donations and endowments, and a further £200m from the government (mostly school fees for children of soldiers and diplomats serving overseas). In no other European country do private schools maintain such a tight grip on the ruling elite. This may go at least part of the way to explaining why the UK is so far down international rankings for social mobility and educational attainment.

In their book, *What Do We Know and What Should We Do About Social Mobility?*, Professors Lee Elliot Major and Stephen Machin trace the rise of economic inequality and the accompanying fall in social mobility that has afflicted the UK since the 1980s. In today's Britain, downward mobility is more likely than upward. 'In 2006, 64 per cent of 30- and 40-year-olds equalled or exceeded their fathers' earnings in real terms at the same ages. By 2019 this fell dramatically to 44 per cent. The majority now earned less. The dream of just doing better, let alone climbing the social ladder, is disappearing.'[37] And the public is noticing this decline in life chances.

A recent study by Ipsos Mori found that the proportion of people who believe there is equality of opportunity in Britain has fallen from 53 per cent in 2010 to 35 per cent in 2020. David Cameron's mantra of 'it's where you're going to, not where you're from that counts' is ringing increasingly hollow. Many international studies have confirmed the UK's low standing on income mobility. OECD figures published in 2018 show the UK lying 18th out of 23 developed countries measured for income mobility. In 2020, the World Economic Forum concluded that the world's top five countries for income mobility were all from Scandinavia. The UK lagged behind every other G7 industrialised country apart from Italy and the USA.

The main factor in determining a country's degree of social mobility is its overall level of economic inequality. Sociologists have proved this with a graph called the *Great Gatsby* curve, named after F Scott Fitzgerald's classic novel set in the so-called Gilded Age of 1920s America, an era defined by its extremes of wealth and poverty. The more unequal a country, the lower its level of social mobility. In relatively equal Finland, it takes a poor child an average of three generations for his descendants to reach the national average income, compared with five generations in the relatively unequal UK and USA, and nine generations in Brazil.

At the end of the day, our attitude to private schools is inextricably bound up with our attitude to society. Are we comfortable living in a country where the children of key workers who kept the UK going during the pandemic have little to no chance of benefiting from an elite education, and an ever-decreasing chance of owning their own homes or even earning as much as their low-paid parents? Or do we want to live in a fairer society where equality of opportunity is a reality, not a mirage?

The American political philosopher John Rawls specialised in social justice. He devised a theoretical scenario he believed would encourage us to create a just society. He called it the 'veil of ignorance' and it worked like this. Imagine that you are about to be born into a society, but you have no idea whether your parents will be rich or poor. Together with other ignorant people in the same situation, your task is to draw up the society's ground rules for equality of opportunity, before you pass through the veil to take up your randomly allocated place in the social pecking order.

Rawls believed that, under these theoretical conditions, most of us, being risk averse, would probably opt for a society that promotes real equality of opportunity, because it would mean that if, at birth, we ended up on the wrong side of the tracks, we would still have a good chance of attaining upward social mobility during the rest of our life. Only high-risk gamblers would choose the USA model where the odds are stacked against the poor improving their lot. Faced with this choice, the majority of people would surely prefer the Nordic model of social solidarity and genuine equality of opportunity. As Kate Pickett, co-author of the best-selling book, *The Spirit Level,* once said in an interview: 'If you want to live the American dream, go and live in Denmark.'

On this measure, it is clear that Britain is not yet a socially just society, as even David Cameron admitted in a speech to the Conservative party conference in 2015: 'Britain has the lowest social mobility in the developed world. Here the salary you earn is more linked to what your father got paid than in any other major country. I'm sorry, for us

Conservatives, the party of aspiration, we cannot accept that. We know that education is the springboard to opportunity'.

I don't agree with Stewart Maconie that we should turn our private schools into Aldis and nail bars, but I do support Alan Bennett's view that private education is not fair. By implication, we British, who believe so much in fair play (or say we do), need to overcome our normative dissonance and do something about it. As Tony Parsons puts it: 'We need to change the blight of our educational apartheid for our own sakes. Because if it persists, then this land will not be a pleasant place to live for anyone. Never underestimate the bitterness of those who are left at the bottom of the pile, with no way up or out.'[38]

There are two ways to go: reduce the supply of private education or cut the demand for it. Abolition goes down the supply route, and while it would be the quickest way of addressing the problem, it's never going to happen because the opposition—from the right-wing media, parliament and the City of London—would be too strong. Scrapping charitable status would be an attack on the demand for private education because it would push up the cost of school fees. But, while it might be more achievable politically, it's not worth doing for three reasons. First, it would remove any incentive for private schools to award full scholarships to children like Kiran Samrai. Scholarships may be a charitable fig leaf for the private sector, but for the disadvantaged kids who benefit from them they represent an escape route from poverty. Secondly, there are private schools for children with special needs and special talents (e.g., musicians). They continue to survive only thanks to their charitable status. Finally, the richest schools, such as Eton and Harrow, would be able to carry on as private enterprises with no public benefit obligations.

But, if we don't abolish them or remove their charitable status, what can we do? My solution is to leave the supply of private education as it is. This way we don't need to waste time arguing about freedom of parental choice. I would instead suggest that the best way forward is to choke off demand, by making private schools less attractive as guaranteed paths to glittering prizes. The green shoots of social justice have already been sprouting in one of the two most sought-after universities on the planet.

In 2016, Lady Margaret Hall in Oxford started to offer candidates from state schools a foundation year, to prepare them for a full undergraduate degree course. The college accepted lower than normal grades from promising applicants. Of the first two years' intake, eight out of 10 students went on to graduate from Oxford. According to former Lady Margaret Hall principal, Alan Rusbridger: 'Creating a more level admissions playing field is not dumbing down but helping up. Foundation years are a very powerful tool in allowing extraordinarily talented and committed young people to have an Oxford education.'[39]

The university is now running two programmes aimed at ensuring that, by the end of 2023, one in four Oxford undergraduate students who come from the UK will be from what the university describes as 'under-represented backgrounds,' based on various factors such as ethnicity, quality of state school and family income. In fact, there's now a contest between Oxford colleges to claim the highest percentage of state school students. Leading the pack is Mansfield College, which from 2018-20 accepted 94 per cent of its UK students from state schools, compared with 68 per cent across the wider university in 2020, up from 62 per cent in 2019.

Of course, the independent schools are alarmed by this development, as it leaves their pupils competing for a reduced number of Oxbridge and Russell Group places. Why pay for an expensive education for your child if they would stand a better chance of getting into a top university by going through the state system? The headmaster of Stowe School, Anthony Wallersteiner, accused Oxbridge of engaging in social engineering to reduce the number of privately educated pupils entering their hallowed portals. The Headmasters' Conference, which represents some of the leading private schools, warned that Oxbridge access targets might 'discriminate against young people based on the class they were born into.'[40] The same argument could be used to describe the unfairness of the system that has been in place up to now, except that the millions of young people discriminated against for more than two centuries have been from the working class. And given that talent is equally distributed among all children, regardless of class, how could it be discriminatory for Oxford to seek to increase the percentage of state school students when they represent the overwhelming majority of the population?

Instead of listening to the private sector's self-serving justifications, we need to continue striving for fairness until fully 93 per cent of places in our top universities are reserved for state school pupils. Even then, the universities need to go out of their way to admit candidates not only from state schools in affluent areas, but also from deprived neighbourhoods. This is where contextual admissions criteria come in. They involve assessing an applicant's socio-economic background, where they grew up and the quality of the state school they attended.

To help this process, I would suggest that the works of fiction otherwise known as 'personal statements' should include an obligatory section describing the applicant's social and economic background, including their parents' educational background and occupations. The advantage of using universities as agents of social change is that they are independent and so can make decisions on admissions quotas without any reference to parliament or the tabloids.

While MPs are beholden to their constituents and often bullied by tabloid headlines, vice-chancellors and their academic staff are self-governing and free to pursue the moral high ground.

In his novel, *1984,* Old Etonian George Orwell invented the concept of 'double think.' This meant holding two completely contradictory ideas in one's mind simultaneously, without realising the contradiction. The British tolerance for private education is a good example of this act of mental contortionism. The following propositions are incompatible: 'Britain is a meritocracy' and: 'Private education gives you an edge in the struggle for academic excellence and the best jobs.' You don't need to be Sherlock Holmes to realise that they cannot both be true. If we want to make a reality of the first proposition, then there's only one way forward. It's time to turn our seven per cent problem into a 93 per cent solution.

CHAPTER 9

TO SIR, WITH LOVE

Teachers deserve more TLC

Just eight words from George Bernard Shaw's play *Man and Superman* have been used to taunt teachers the world over, since it was first performed in 1903. 'He who can, does. He who cannot, teaches.' It's the ultimate put-down for those who choose a career in the classroom, but one which is palpably false, as millions of parents discovered when forced by the pandemic to educate their own children at home. Even before Covid, we've always recognised the role of teachers in inspiring pupils to realise their potential, and in some cases their dreams. There are plenty of fictional examples from film and literature. In *Billy Elliot,* the eponymous miner's son is encouraged by the Julie Walters character, Sandra Wilkinson, to become a professional ballet dancer. In *The Dead Poets Society,* eccentric English teacher John Keating, played by Robin Williams, uses unorthodox methods to bring poetry to life for his cynical male charges. After multiple trials and tribulations, Sydney Poitier eventually wins the hearts and minds of his pupils at a tough East End school in *To Sir, With Love.*

Teachers are not, however, always portrayed in a positive light. In the Netflix series *Breaking Bad,* Walter White morphs from a mild-mannered chemistry teacher into a ruthless drugs kingpin, while in the series of blockbuster adventure films that began with *Raiders of the Lost Ark*, Indiana Jones neglects his students in favour of adrenalin-fuelled field trips to the wilds of Peru, Egypt, Mexico, and India.

In real life, there are indeed some famous examples of artists turning their backs on the teaching profession. Sting gave up teaching to form The Police, one of whose most successful songs was about a teacher having a taboo relationship with a female student. Playwright Samuel Beckett might never have written *Waiting for Godot* had he instead waited for a promotion as a teacher at Belfast's prestigious Campbell College. The head teacher expressed his disappointment at Beckett's decision to quit his job, describing the school's pupils as representing 'the cream of Ulster.' Beckett disdainfully replied with the immortal line: 'Yes, rich and thick.'

But, for those who stay the course in the teaching trade, there are vicarious rewards aplenty in the form of high-achieving students. Imagine how the Greek philosopher Aristotle must have felt when the boy he tutored between the ages of 13 and 16 went on to conquer most of the known ancient world. Alexander the Great doubtless made good use of the insights into medicine, science, literature and philosophy which he gleaned from a superstar teacher who was himself a pupil of Plato.

When 40-year-old French teacher and mother-of-four Bridget Auzière indulged a precocious 15-year-old pupil by the name of Emmanuel, could she have guessed that he would one day become the president of the republic and her second husband? When drama teacher Philip Burton fostered the theatrical talents of a boy from a poor South Wales family, he helped to propel one of Britain's greatest actors of the twentieth century to fame and fortune in Hollywood. In return the future star paid him the compliment of taking his surname, so that Elizabeth Taylor married Richard Burton, not Richard Jenkins.

The very best teachers can change not just single lives, but hundreds or even thousands. In 2018 Andria Zafirakou won the *Global Teacher Prize*, worth £1m. An arts and textiles teacher at Alperton community school in Brent, one of London's most deprived boroughs, she goes well beyond her contractual obligations, driving students home when there are gangs waiting for them at the school gates, buying a uniform for a pupil whose family cannot afford one and running weekend and holiday arts clubs for children who need to escape from crowded or violent homes.

In her book, pointedly titled *Those Who Can, Teach*, she describes how her own experience as the daughter of Greek immigrants allowed her to identify with the diverse backgrounds of her students. To make pupils and their parents feel more at ease, she learned everyday greetings in dozens of languages. For her, teaching is not just a job, it's a way of life: 'We teach because we have to, because there is nothing else we would rather do. It is hard to put into words that golden moment when you see a light flicker on behind the eyes of the student who has been struggling to understand a concept for weeks, or the student who softens after months of putting on a hard exterior. Yet these are the moments that make everything else worthwhile. There is no feeling like it, to know that you have made a difference, that you have inspired a young person to do or be better. That, for us, is everything.'[1]

In the USA, another outstanding teacher, Jaime Escalante, won such renown for teaching calculus to poor Latino students in Los Angeles that his exploits were celebrated in the 1988 Oscar-nominated film *Stand and Deliver*. An immigrant from Bolivia who spoke no English when he arrived in America, he played a leading role in gaining an exceptional pass rate for his school in the country's toughest maths exam. For him, a pupil's success or failure depended on how high or low the academic bar was set: 'If we expect kids to be losers they will be losers; if we expect them to be winners they will be winners. They rise, or fall, to the level of the expectations of those around them, especially their parents and their teachers.'

A colleague who grew up in one of the poorest parts of Birmingham told me that when, as a teenager, he had a minor run-in with the police, one of the strictest teachers in his school took him into his office and nearly broke down in tears as he explained how much it meant to him that bright children from poor backgrounds should use their educational opportunities as a means of escaping from poverty. 'He told me that helping kids like me was the reason he went into teaching, and that was why he was so upset when he thought I might be risking my future at school by getting into trouble with the police.'

Given the generally positive image of fictional and real-life teachers, you would expect them to enjoy a high social status, and this is borne out in the UK by the latest research. The Varkey Foundation, which also sponsors the *Global Teacher Prize*, surveyed 35,000 people in 35 countries for their *2018 Global Teacher Status Index*.[2] Since the previous study in 2013, the status of UK teachers rose relative to other countries. In Europe only Greece values teachers more highly than Britain (globally teachers have the highest status in China, while Brazil holds them in the lowest esteem). Yet the study found that most people in the UK put teachers on a par with social workers and nurses. Only three per cent compared them with doctors.

When it came to pay, those surveyed significantly overestimated the starting salary for a secondary school teacher, thinking it was £29,000 pounds (in 2018 it was £24,000). Respondents thought a fair salary for such teachers would be £31,500 (teachers in other European countries earn far more than in the UK. In Germany, for example, a new teacher earns £50,000 and in Spain the salary is £36,000). Perhaps this explains why, despite their relatively high social status, only 23 per cent of British parents would encourage their children to become teachers (down on the 2013 figure of 26 per cent).

Judging by the ongoing crisis in recruiting and retaining teachers, most children are listening to their parents and spurning a career in the classroom. Despite the government pumping millions into a national recruitment campaign and a series of incentive measures, the picture remains bleak. Underpinning the problem is a double demographic whammy. On the one hand, there are fewer people of the right age group available to become teachers. In 2019 the number of 21-year-olds fell to its lowest in a decade. On the other, the number of pupils per teacher is rising, particularly in secondary schools. In the three years to 2022 they grew by 17 per cent. Overall, by 2025, there will be 1m extra school children, compared with 2010.

The teacher shortages are particularly acute in the so-called STEM subjects (Science, Technology, Engineering and Mathematics). Students with degrees in these subjects can often find better-paid and less stressful jobs in other sectors. From 2012 to 2017 English schools met only 68 per cent of their recruitment targets for new computing teachers. From 2019-20 the targets for secondary school teachers fell short by 59 per cent for design and technology, 57 per cent for physics and 34 per cent for maths.

The reasons behind these shortfalls are widely recognised. To begin with, in recent years, graduate pay in the private sector has been higher than ever before. *The Daily Telegraph* reported in January 2019 that starting salaries in investment banks were around £60,000, compared with £45,000 in law firms and £44,000 working in management roles for supermarket chains.[3] By contrast, trainee teachers have to spend an extra year and more than £9,000 to study for the Postgraduate Certificate in Education (PGCE) qualification that most need in order to start their teaching careers on a starting salary of £28,000 per year. The result is that new teachers are paid about 20 per cent less than the average graduate trainee.

Another factor is the growth in the number of international teaching jobs, which tempts more and more teachers away from the UK. Most international schools teach in English, giving UK teachers a native speaker advantage in the jobs market. ISC Research, which provides data on international schools, predicts that the number of international schoolteachers will grow from 506,800 in 2019 to 917,000 in 2028. In 2018, *The Economist* cited the case of Ewa, a modern languages teacher who left the UK to work at a private school in Dubai, earning three times as much as she did in London. 'Perks include free flights home, accommodation, private health insurance and even a furniture allowance. Five years after qualifying as a teacher she is head of her year. Would she return? Her "heart beats for London" but living there "on a teacher's salary can be really difficult." So, not soon.'[4] Writing in *The New Statesman*, Laura McInerney observed that in 2015 the number of teachers leaving to teach abroad—18,000—exceeded the number of new teachers trained that year at UK universities.[5]

In his book, *Recruiting Teachers,* Simon Hepburn argues that teaching in UK state schools has become an increasingly unappealing job. Between 2005 and 2017, teacher pay in England plummeted by 10 per cent in real terms, according to the Organization for Economic Cooperation and Development (OECD).[6]

Yet if teaching were a more satisfying job, declining real pay would not be such a disincentive. But, in recent years, the job has become more and more stressful. A study by the Nuffield Foundation, a think tank based at University College London, analysed data from more than 30,000 teachers and education professionals in England at different stages between 1992 and 2018. They found that around five per cent of teachers say they have a chronic mental health problem caused by the job—up from only one per cent in the 1990s.[7]

The proportion of education professionals using antidepressant medication (also five per cent) has increased from the one per cent recorded in the 2000s. Many respondents cited understaffing and an increased workload as contributing factors to their poor mental health. The strains of teaching during the pandemic have almost certainly accentuated these negative trends, but even before Covid, teachers in England came top in a stress league table compiled by the OECD. Around 38 per cent of its teachers feel stressed much of the time. That's more than double the OECD average.

University College London professor John Jerrim observed: 'The teaching profession in England is currently in the midst of a crisis and one potential reason why it's struggling to recruit and retain enough teachers is due to the pressures of the job. It has long been known that teaching is a stressful and challenging career and we wanted to see if the mental health and well-being of teachers had improved or declined, especially in light of government promises to ease the burden on the teaching profession.'[8] The latter would clearly seem to be the case.

According to Mary Bousted, the joint General Secretary of the National Education Union, the main stress factor is excessive time spent on lesson preparation, marking and admin tasks. The result is that teachers work more unpaid overtime than any other profession in the country. She also cites overbearing levels of scrutiny, oversight and monitoring that mean teachers in England are watched more than any of their OECD peers. The union claims that fear of Ofsted, the body responsible for inspecting and regulating schools, creates a climate of compliance that robs teachers of their professionalism.

Francis Gilbert trains teachers on the post-graduate secondary English programme at Goldsmiths, University of London. He agrees that there is too much external evaluation of classroom performance: 'Teachers often work in fear that they will be judged as failing by the inspectorate or even by someone acting out the role of inspector—school senior leadership teams frequently run Mocksteds, where teachers undergo a mock Ofsted.'

In January 2023, Ruth Perry, the head teacher at Caversham Primary School in Reading, took her own life while waiting for an Ofsted report that downgraded her school to 'inadequate.' Her family said they had no doubt that her death had been caused by the 'intolerable' pressure put on her by the Ofsted inspection.

In addition to excessive scrutiny by Ofsted, Francis Gilbert also criticises increasingly unrealistic expectations on the part of parents and students, due to the marketisation of education, with teachers reduced to mere 'customer service agents' charged with delivering a product in the form of a good grade, rather than improving pupils' capacity to learn. 'I know of a brilliant, experienced teacher who was verbally abused and threatened at a parents' evening by an angry mother who felt that this teacher should have 'got' a better result for her child. The onus has shifted away from students to work for themselves and instead has been placed on the teacher to do the work for the student.'[9]

In her award-winning book, *Some Kids I Taught, and What They Taught Me*, teacher and author Kate Clanchy suspects that unrealistic expectations are not the only reason why parents so often take teachers to task. She thinks that gender and social class also play a major role: 'People feel free to set about a teacher in a way they never would a doctor or a lawyer. For teachers have a lower social standing than other professionals. This isn't just because we are paid less, as I found out when I entered the even less well remunerated, but far more prestigious, profession of writing. And it isn't just because of the messy, practical nature of teachers' work, either: laymen do not tell a vet how to go about birthing calves, or a gynaecologist where to poke. It may be because so many teachers are women; or perhaps because we work with poor children; and it is certainly because so few of us are posh ourselves (teaching has always been the profession of first resort for graduates from working-class backgrounds).'[10]

Some teachers also point the finger at the government

for what they allege is a disgraceful lack of respect for their profession. Writing in *The New Statesman,* Jumbo Chan, a teacher and councillor from North London, claimed there was a damaging tendency to micromanage: 'Masses of paperwork, administrative tasks and tick-box exercises are carried out, merely to satiate bureaucratic whims. Together with the pace of centrally imposed curricular and structural changes, many teachers find a job that should be inspiring, grinding.'[11]

It doesn't help that so many of the country's 22,000 state schools are in a bad physical condition. A repair survey published in May 2021 by the Department of Education confirmed years of complaints by teachers and parents of crumbling and leaking buildings, in some cases riddled with asbestos, and temporary cabins becoming a long-term solution. Fire safety is a particular concern, with only one in three new schools fitted with sprinklers in recent years.

According to the report, remedial work will cost £11.4bn, including £2.5bn needed for electrical and IT repairs, with another £2bn earmarked for fixing boilers and air conditioning, and an additional £1.5bn for roofs, windows and walls.[12] No wonder so many potential teachers opt for the comforts of an air-conditioned modern office instead of a clapped-out classroom. Not that decrepit buildings are a new phenomenon.

In her book, *Respectable,* journalist Lynsey Hanley recalls her half-empty secondary school in one of the poorest parts of Birmingham: 'When it was new, the campus must have looked like the sign of a spanking new social order: it had a swimming pool, a theatre-style assembly hall, a craft and technology block, thousands of new books, the works. By 1990, the year I turned fourteen, it looked old before its time. The school buildings, built to serve twice the number, felt like half-abandoned husks. The school as a whole felt 50, not 20, years-old, with classrooms unused, walls unadorned with project work. In these ghostly rooms, from nine o'clock, we would have a lot of half-hour lessons during which nothing useful would be imparted or absorbed.'[13]

Given the relatively meagre pay, an often-run-down work environment and a punishing workload, maybe we shouldn't be shocked that so many newly qualified teachers leave the occupation prematurely. More than 25 per cent do so within two years of qualifying, rising to 40 per cent within a decade. This haemorrhage of talent creates a vicious circle, because in England and Wales teachers qualify as teachers rather than, for example, maths teachers. As staffing shortages bite, the first impact is that teachers are deployed from subjects with adequate numbers to those where there are unfilled vacancies.

In the BBC documentary, *The School,* a PE teacher told the programme what it was like to be switched to the role of maths teacher: 'I find it tough, so they find it tough. I've got to keep teaching myself before I can teach them.'[14] The stress generated by teaching a subject outside of your comfort zone is another factor pushing these square peg teachers out of the classroom door, into private tutoring, early retirement or another occupation altogether.

It doesn't have to be this way. There are countries in Europe where recruiting and retaining teachers is not a problem. All we need to do is *Look and Learn,* to borrow the title of an illustrated weekly children's magazine my parents used to buy for me, along with *World of Wonder*. And the place we have most to learn from is Finland, the world's happiest country, and Europe's most consistent top performer in international league tables measuring educational attainment.

There are many things about Finland's education system that stand in stark contrast to the UK. School starts at age seven, to allow children more time to develop creative and social skills. 'We believe children under seven are not ready to start school' said one day care centre head. 'They need time to play and be physically active. It's a time for creativity.'[15] At day care centres, which are modestly priced and free for poor families, the emphasis is not on maths, reading or writing, but on creative play, and forming relationships with other children.

Schools in Finland are small by UK standards—a third have 50 or fewer pupils, and only four per cent have more than 500 pupils. Class sizes range from 15 to 30 students and according to the most recent OECD *Education at a Glance* report, there is one teacher to every nine students, compared with an OECD average of 13. Children have an average of 20 hours of lessons per week, and homework is relatively light. There are free school meals for everyone, regardless of family income, and each school also provides healthcare and psychological counselling.

There are no standardised tests—the only national exam takes place at the end of upper secondary education when most students are 18 years of age. Instead, students are graded individually, using a system created by their teacher, who may stay with them for as long as six years. The emphasis is always on learning and problem solving rather than testing and ranking.

Unlike the UK, the independent school sector is tiny—just two per cent of pupils attend them—and private tutoring is almost unheard of. The majority of schools are publicly funded comprehensives, meaning they are not only non-selective but there is also no such thing as academic streaming. Instead, each school has at least one special needs teacher to help pupils with learning difficulties. There are no school league tables, and schools are encouraged to cooperate with each other rather than compete, with the aim of sharing best practices and new ideas for improved learning.

Regional differences in the quality of schools are very small. In 2013, a report by the OECD's Programme for International Student Assessment (PISA) found that differences among schools in Finland accounted for only 7.7 per cent in variation between student performance, against an OECD average of 42 per cent.[16] As a result, most parents send their children to the local school, though they are free to choose any other establishment within their municipality.

Teachers spend an average of three hours a day in the classroom, spread over four lessons, each lasting 45 minutes. The rest of their time is devoted to lesson preparation, assessment, curriculum planning and liaising with colleagues on school matters. There are no Ofsted-like inspections and no heated debates on school governance and structure of the kind that seem to obsess the UK, as it compares the merits of free schools, academies and grammars, none of which exist in Finland.

Little wonder then that teaching is a high-status profession in Finland. Annually only one in ten applicants are accepted to study to become a primary school teacher (working with seven to 13-year-olds). In 2011, the University of Helsinki received 2,100 applications for 120 places on its teacher training course. Schoolteachers at both primary and upper secondary level have to complete a five-year master's course, while kindergarten teachers need a three year bachelor's degree to qualify. Like all public education in Finland, university is free of charge, so trainee teachers do not accumulate debt while studying.

The average salary of £36,000 is not the main reason why young people become teachers in Finland. Just as important are factors like high social prestige, professional autonomy and the ethos of teaching as a service to society and the public good. Young Finns see teaching as a career on a par with other professions where people work independently and rely on scientific knowledge and skills gained at university.

According to the OECD, Finland has succeeded in creating a virtuous circle to train and retain high-quality teachers: 'High status and good working conditions—small classes, adequate support for counsellors and special needs teachers, a voice in school decisions, low levels of discipline problems, high levels of professional autonomy—create large pools of applicants, leading to highly selective and intensive teacher-preparation programmes. This in turn leads to success in the early years of teaching, relative stability of the teaching workforce, success in teaching (of which the PISA results are only one example) and a continuation of the high status of teaching.'

Of course, there are many differences between Finland and the UK, including social values, history and size. Nevertheless, we should try to emulate the respect that Finns have for the professionalism and autonomy of teachers. One way to do this is for us to start thinking of teachers in the same way we do for doctors. The medical profession has a high degree of independence and self-assessment. Politicians never make statements criticising doctors, and newspaper columnists rarely describe them as lazy lefties.

We should be putting teachers on a pedestal, instead of using them as political punch bags, lectured far too often on how to do their jobs by practitioners of two of the country's least respected professions: politicians and journalists. This means shifting accountability away from make-or-break school inspections, high stakes testing, simplistic grading and divisive league tables, and towards peer-based assessment and self-regulation of teachers by teachers. Student grants or bursaries for teacher training courses, clearer career structures and higher salaries at all levels would also go a long way to raising the attractiveness of a teaching career for graduates, as well as retaining those who are already doing it.

As in Finland, schools should be encouraged to cooperate with each other rather than compete, and teachers should be able to experiment, within well-defined limits, to find better ways of learning. Research and development are vital in all sectors, and education is no exception. Teachers should be allowed to take career breaks to refresh and update their specialist knowledge, learn new pedagogical skills and do research projects.

Unfortunately, there are few signs that any UK government is about to grant more autonomy to the teaching profession. On the contrary, the Department of Education is proposing to shake up teacher training by requiring a more stringent accreditation process that critics argue would reduce capacity across 30 training providers, with several universities likely to pull out altogether, leading to 10,000 fewer training places. One way to reverse this top-down tendency would be to equip the Chartered College of Teaching or a similar standard-setting body with the powers to scrutinise and ultimately veto any decisions put forward by the Department of Education. This new House of Lords for education would establish a level of consensus which should ultimately lead to balanced, meaningful and useful reforms.

Dame Alison Peacock, the Chief Executive Officer of the Chartered College of Teaching, believes the pandemic has strengthened the case for putting a stop to teacher-bashing: 'I believe there is a really positive opportunity now for society to understand and value the importance of teaching. This is why when some in the media and prominent politicians criticise our efforts we respond with disappointment and incredulity. I am not saying the profession is immune to criticism. We know that there will be lessons to learn from all of this. This outbreak has led to discussions regarding the relationship between home and in-school learning, the role of technology in education, the experience of children who cannot access school and the very nature of education. These are discussions we must have. We cannot simply return to business as usual. However, nothing is accomplished by criticising our teachers during a global emergency.'[17]

Sadly, this advice has long been ignored by many of the world's most successful musicians. In stark contrast to the world of cinema, popular music has consistently failed to sing the praises of teachers. Songs are either about teenage crushes (*Don't Stand So Close To Me* from the Police, Van Halen's *Hot For Teacher*, and *Teacher I Need You* by Elton John) or are downright negative. Prime examples of the latter are Alice Cooper's *Schools Out* and Pink Floyd's *Another Brick In The Wall*.

Recent research by the Varkey Foundation appears to show a correlation between a country's level of esteem for its teachers, and its results in the OECD's PISA tests. The higher the esteem, the better the results.[18] Improving our teachers' social status, it seems, is one of the key routes to providing a better education for the majority of pupils who attend state schools. But this will only happen when politicians, many of whom send their own children to private schools, stop interfering with teachers and let them regulate themselves, as doctors do via the British Medical Association and the General Medical Council. We need to take a leaf out of Pink Floyd's book, or rather album, and send a clear message to the government: 'Hey, Minister, leave them teachers alone!'.

CHAPTER 10

NEVER MIND THE THREE RS, WHAT ABOUT THE FOUR CS?

Reforming the school curriculum

When I went to school in the 1960s, great emphasis was laid on the three Rs: Reading, Writing and Arithmetic. Yes, I know that only the first subject starts with an R, but that's because the man who coined the phrase was himself illiterate, believing that Writing and Arithmetic both began with the letter R (making him an alliterative illiterate). Sir William Curtis made his fortune selling sea biscuits to the Royal Navy, hence his nickname, 'Sir Billy Biscuit.' His lack of literacy did not, however, prevent him from rising to the heights of the British establishment, as he became both Lord Mayor and MP for the City of London.

His immortal contribution to defining the academic gold standard came in 1795, as part of a speech he gave in the House of Commons during a debate on education.

Responding to talk about the importance of Latin and Greek, Sir William insisted that: 'What children need is the three Rs: Readin', 'Ritin' and 'Rithetic.' For my part, I think that in a world of climate change, post-truth politics and artificial intelligence, modern children are in urgent need of another cluster of letters: the four Cs. Creativity, Critical Thinking, Citizenship and Climate Change all deserve a much higher priority in our school curriculum. To find out why, let's take them one at a time, starting with Creativity.

Oxford economist Daniel Susskind opens his optimistically titled book, *A World Without Work,* with what one observer dubbed 'the Parable of Horseshit.'[1] It is more commonly described as the Great Manure Crisis of the 1890s. Big cities like New York and London had long relied on hundreds of thousands of horses for all kinds of transport, from cabs and wagons to buses and fire engines. There were fears that manure would pile up in the streets to the height of a third storey building (a case perhaps of the shit hitting not only the fan but the ceiling as well). In the end, the problem was solved by the invention of the internal combustion engine, which meant that, by 1912, New York had more cars than horses. The last horse-drawn tram was decommissioned in 1917, marking the end of the crisis.

Taking the glass-half-full approach, this was a prime example of how technology can solve seemingly intractable problems. But Susskind prefers a much darker interpretation, first suggested by the Nobel Prize winning economist Wassily Leontief: 'What he saw instead was how a new technology, the combustion engine, had taken a creature that, for millennia, had played a central role in economic life, not only in cities but on farms and fields, and in only a matter of decades had banished it to the side lines. What technological progress had done to horses, he said, it would eventually do to human beings as well: drive us out of work. What cars and tractors were to them, he thought, computers and robots would do to us.'[2]

Of course, horses have not vanished from the face of the earth. They are still used for riding and racing, but, to all intents and purposes, they now play a very minor role in the economy. For humans, the impact of new technology will no doubt be less devastating, but the direction of travel is nevertheless very clear. Autonomous cars, lorries and delivery drones will put millions of drivers out of work. Researchers claim that a baby born after 2022 will never need to take a driving test.

Supermarkets are already employing far fewer cashiers thanks to labour saving, self-service check outs. But it may not be long before the country's remaining 270,000 till-staff, most of them women, could find themselves checked out of a job. Following the example of Amazon, the main UK food retailers are heavily investing in so-called smart supermarkets, which have no place for human cashiers. Instead, customers enter the store using a mobile app to identify themselves, cameras then record their purchases and payment is made automatically online with customers receiving a receipt via email. As well as saving on staff costs, the new system makes shop lifting and skimming by dishonest employees much more difficult, if not impossible, representing a potential annual saving to the industry of £5.5bn.[3]

In the building trade, a robot called Sam100 can lay more than 3,000 bricks in the time it takes a skilled bricklayer to place 600. The leading UK construction company, Balfour Beatty, has predicted that by 2050 its building sites will be human free, with robotic cranes and diggers controlled remotely, as drones fly overhead to monitor progress.[4] In America, several companies are already building experimental homes with 3D printers. Architect Andrew Logan predicts that, in another two decades: 'You will be able to buy a piece of land and print your own home using an app on your phone.' Logan Architecture uses robots to build walls by means of a nozzle suspended from an overhead gantry. Software guides the machine as it pipes parallel beads of cement, like toothpaste on a brush, layer on layer. The whole process is overseen by just one person, described as 'a guy with his feet up babysitting a machine.'[5]

In 2017, the Harper Adams agricultural university in Shropshire pioneered the first farm in the world to successfully plant, tend and harvest a crop without a single person ever setting foot in a field. From sowing the seeds to picking the grain, human workers were replaced with automated machines operated from a control room. The project, called Hands Free Hectare, yielded 4.5 tons of spring barley in its first harvest (the project team celebrated by making and consuming a batch of 'Hands-Free' beer.)[6]

In May 2023, the telecoms giant BT (British Telecom) announced plans to make 55,000 staff redundant by 2030. The company said that one in five of the job losses would come in the customer service sector, and were due to technological advances, especially in the field of Artificial Intelligence (AI).

AI is also encroaching into service industries such as banking, medicine and law. Cancers are detected, legal documents drafted, and loans approved by algorithms. As Susskind explains, automation will be a gradual but steady process: 'Machines will not do everything in the future, but they will do more. And as they slowly, but relentlessly, take on more and more tasks, human beings will be forced to retreat to an ever-shrinking set of activities. Farmers and factory workers are still needed, despite automation. Their jobs have not entirely vanished. But the number of workers needed to do those jobs has fallen in both cases, sometimes precipitously, even though these sectors produce more than ever before. We should be worried not about a world without *any* work to do, as some predict, but a world without *enough* work for everyone to do'.[7]

The kind of work most likely to resist the rise of the robots is, not surprisingly, that which requires the human touch. Fitness instructors, hairdressers, nurses, social workers, schoolteachers and police officers are just some of the jobs that we would prefer humans to do, even if robots were technically capable of doing them. Sceptics argue that technology also creates new jobs. They point to the recently created roles of search engine optimisers, data scientists, cloud computing specialists, digital marketing consultants and mobile app developers. There are more cutting-edge vacancies in the pipeline.

According to a recently published government innovation strategy, Britain's industrial future lies with seven broad 'technology families:' advanced materials and manufacturing; artificial intelligence, digital and advanced computing; bioinformatics and genomics; engineering biology; electronics, photonics and quantum; energy and environment technologies; and robotics and smart machines.[8] The problem is that few unemployed supermarket workers or lorry drivers will have either the qualifications or the learning aptitudes to secure jobs in these sunrise industries.

The inevitable result of technological progress will be unprecedentedly high levels of unemployment. This danger poses a double threat to the stability of democratic societies. Mass unemployment and extremes of wealth and poverty can lead to populist leaders taking power. In Weimar Germany, an unemployment rate of 24 per cent helped propel Hitler to the Chancellery. The other problem is that robots and algorithms don't get paid for the work they do, which means they don't spend anything either. A robot doesn't need to eat, furnish a home or go on holiday. Humans, on the other hand, are consumers as well as producers. While investment in automation allows firms to produce more efficiently, it also reduces demand for goods and services because the workers who lose their jobs also lose their purchasing power.

So where does our education system fit into all this? On the one hand, it's a safe bet that the best paid jobs will continue to go to science and maths students and those with coding skills. On the other, schools also need to prepare pupils for careers such as teaching, social work and the care sector. These kinds of jobs may often be less well remunerated, but they have the advantage of being harder to automate.

Schools should give more priority to arts subjects, because it turns out that the best kind of jobs for keeping robots and algorithms at bay are those that require a high degree of creativity. These range from tech-related roles such as software developers, gaming designers and biochemical engineers to more traditional creative professions like architects, musicians, actors, artists and dancers as well as those working in fashion, film, television, advertising and marketing. Collectively they are known as the creative industries. In 2019, the year before the pandemic, they employed more than 2m people and contributed nearly £116bn to the UK economy.[9] That's more than the automotive, aerospace, life sciences and oil and gas sectors combined.

In the period from 2010 to 2019, the creative industries grew nearly three times as fast as the UK average. A 2015 study found that only one in six creative jobs had a high risk of being automated, compared with one in three in non-creative industries.[10] That's good news for the country, because the researchers estimated that as many as 24 per cent of all UK jobs had a high probability of being classified as creative. Moreover, they found that new technology was often a handy tool for the sector's workers, rather than a means of replacing them. For example, architects use sophisticated software to visualise their plans and musicians can experiment with new programs to create different sounds and rhythms.

Even for those without creative jobs, or indeed jobs of any kind, artistic hobbies can help to significantly improve their mental health, according to a ground-breaking study carried out by researchers at University College London (UCL) for the BBC. The study, involving 50,000 people, explored how creative activities like painting, pottery or playing a musical instrument can help us manage our mood and boost well-being.[11] It identified three main ways in which we use creativity as a coping mechanism to control our emotions. First, it can act as a distraction, avoiding stress by taking our minds off our worries. Secondly, it can be a contemplation tool, giving us the mental space to calmly consider our problems. Finally, it helps to build up our self-esteem and confidence, as we get better at performing our chosen pastime.

Given the proven advantages of creativity for the jobs market, the economy and mental health, it's disappointing to discover that the teaching of arts subjects has been on the slide in English state schools for more than a decade. According to statistics from the Joint Council for Qualifications (JCQ) there was a fall in entries for arts-related GCSEs of 38 per cent from 2010 to 2021.[12] The decline was slightly smaller for A-levels, at 31 per cent.

The figures seem to confirm concerns that creative subjects are being squeezed out by the English Baccalaureate, or EBacc, system, which defines a core set of subjects to be studied until the age of 16. It does not include a single arts subject, prompting fears that it devalues the arts and encourages teachers to steer students away from arts subjects. But it's not only the number of exam entries which is dropping—there are also fewer arts teachers. Arts and design teachers are four per cent down, drama teachers by more than six per cent and music teachers by more than eight per cent.

Britain's scaling back of its commitment to arts education runs against the advice of the Organization for Economic Cooperation and Development (OECD), an international think-tank that counts the UK, Australia and America among its 38 members. According to its Director for Education and Skills, Andreas Schleicher: 'Whatever way you construct your list of 21st century skills, you will always come across creativity: creating new value and looking for outcomes that are innovative, fresh and original. This is all about imagination, inquisitiveness, collaboration, self-discipline.'

Closer to home, the UK's Cultural Learning Alliance argues that it is literally a false economy to skimp on investing in arts education: 'It is essential that we nurture the inventive problem solvers we will need in the future. An education that combines the arts with science, technology, engineering and maths will prepare our young people for the changing needs of the labour market. Leading employers from across the creative industries and beyond are calling for a workforce with both creative and scientific skills.'[13]

* * *

There's an interesting video on You Tube featuring former US President Barack Obama. The title is *You Won't Believe What Obama Says in This Video!*[14] When you press 'play', the charismatic former two-term leader of the free world addresses the camera and solemnly intones that: 'We are entering an era in which our enemies can make it look like anyone is saying anything at any point in time. Even if they would never say those things.' So far so uncontroversial.

But then things take an unexpectedly potty-mouthed turn, seemingly out of character with Obama's trademark eloquence: 'So for instance, they could have me say things like: "President Trump is a total and complete dipshit!"' Alarm bells should start ringing because Obama never uttered these insulting words (even though he probably agrees with them).

The video was made jointly by American film maker Jordan Peele and Buzzfeed as a warning to people not to believe everything they see and hear in the age of the 'deep fake': a type of 'synthetic media' involving images, audio and video that can be manipulated or even wholly generated by Artificial Intelligence in order to create confusion and undermine trust in legitimate sources of information.

The implications for journalists and whistle blowers are obvious. Confronted with incriminating audio, video or photographic evidence, politicians and other power brokers will be able to simply claim that the digital smoking gun is a fake. On the other side of the coin, innocent parties will have their reputations trashed by maliciously fabricated deep fake content designed to undermine their credibility. Speaking truth to power will become increasingly harder while fooling the public will be ever easier.

In her book, *Deep Fakes And The Infocalpyse—What You Urgently Need To Know,* Nina Schick explains how the rapid pace of technological change in recent times has created a tsunami of pseudo information: 'There were four centuries between the invention of the printing press and the development of photography. But, in the last three decades, the Internet, the smartphone and social media have transformed our information environment. By 2023 approximately two-thirds of the world—5.3bn people—will be plugged into this rapidly evolving information environment. The other third will soon join in ... This rapid rate of change has made our information ecosystem ripe for exploitation.'[15]

As well as AI-generated deep fake images, there are also the more traditional low-tech forms of false information that can be either deliberate (disinformation) or unintentionally incorrect (misinformation). There is also malinformation, which is not technically false, since the content is authentic, but the underlying aim is to cause harm. One example of this is revenge porn, when an ex-lover posts intimate photos or video footage of his or her former partner on the Internet without their consent, often causing severe mental suffering to the victim.

The World Economic Forum has described the rapid spread of false information on the Internet as 'digital wildfires.' A good example of such online arsonist activity came in January 2017, when the right-wing website Breitbart published a story about an attack on a church in Dortmund, Germany by a 1,000 strong mob of Islamic extremists. In the short time it took legitimate news outlets to debunk this hoax, it had been shared hundreds of thousands of times on other alt-right sites. To quote the famous saying (ironically itself falsely attributed to Churchill): 'A lie gets halfway around the world before the truth has got its boots on.'

But as the OECD's skills and education director Andreas Schleicher explains, it isn't always a case of disinformation spread by so-called bad actors. The sheer volume of readily available information can be overwhelming: 'In the 20th century if you didn't know the answer to a question you could look it up in an encyclopaedia. You could trust the answer to be true. Today, if you look it up on Google, you get 100,000 answers to your question. Nobody will tell you what is right and what is wrong'. Not even, it seems, that esteemed bastion of British cultural life, whose stated mission since its inception has been to 'inform, educate and entertain.'

Incredibly, in its centenary year, the BBC went on the record as saying that it would, in certain circumstances, devote airtime to proponents of crackpot theories in a bid to combat so-called cancel culture and showcase its impartiality. David Jordan, the BBC's director of editorial policy and standards, told a House of Lords committee: 'Flat Earthers are not going to get as much space as people who believe that the Earth is round, but very occasionally it might be appropriate to interview a flat Earther, and if a lot of people believed in a flat Earth, (then) we would need to address it more than we do at the present time.'[16]

When even the BBC is helping to peddle lunatic theories

that were scientifically disproved more than 2,000 years ago, then we're in a dangerous place. But who are we expecting to come to our rescue? Not the BBC it seems, and certainly not Google, Facebook, Twitter or any of the other runners and riders of Nina Schick's Infocalpyse. Instead, the answer is once again to be found within the plain four walls of the average classroom.

Finland has been taking all forms of fake news very seriously since 2016, when it introduced media literacy and critical thinking as a core component of its national curriculum. When *The Guardian's* Jon Henley visited a secondary school in Helsinki, head teacher Kari Kivenen told him why the country had prioritised these skills: 'The goal is active, responsible citizens and voters. Thinking critically, fact-checking, interpreting and evaluating all the information you receive, wherever it appears, is crucial. We've made it a core part of what we teach, across all subjects.'[17]

In practice, it works like this: when they have a maths lesson, pupils learn how easy it is to lie with statistics. In art, they find out how an image's meaning can be manipulated. When it comes to history, they look at notorious propaganda campaigns from the past, while in language lessons they discover the many ways in which words can be used to mislead, confuse and deceive. The result is that Finland consistently takes pole position in Europe when it comes to combating fake news.

The George Soros-funded Open Society Institute in Sofia runs an annual *Media Literacy Index,* ranking 35 European countries according to their capacity to withstand post-truth and its negative ramifications. In its 2021 edition, the index again put Finland in first place. The UK came in 10th, behind Ireland (fourth), the Netherlands (fifth) and Germany (eighth) but ahead of France (15th) and Italy (21st).[18] The Index compilers wrote that: 'High-quality education and having more and more educated people is a prerequisite for tackling the negative effects of fake news and post-truth.' These sentiments were echoed by the President of the European Research Council, Jean-Pierre Bourguignon, when he addressed the World Economic Forum in 2018: 'We need to train a new generation of critical minds. We must tackle this issue through improved news literacy, and it is the task of our educators and society at large to teach children how to use doubt intelligently and to understand that uncertainty can be quantified and measured.'[19] This means subjecting facts and assertions to a series of searching questions, such as: who produced this information and why? Where was it published? What does it really say? Who is it aimed at? What is it based on? Is there evidence for this, or is it just somebody's opinion?

Back at the Helsinki secondary school, when *The Guardian*'s Jon Henley asked pupils why combating fake news was so important, they came up with some interesting answers.

One student replied: 'You must always fact-check. The number one rule is no Wikipedia and there should always be three or four different and reliable sources.' Another said he had learned much from devising a fake news campaign: 'You end up with wrong numbers on the side of a bus, and voters who believe them.'

* * *

When it comes to protecting democracy, critical thinking isn't the only subject that should be accorded a much higher priority in UK schools. Citizenship education is equally important. It aims to equip children with the knowledge, skills and understanding they need to play a full part in society as active and responsible citizens. Pupils learn about democracy, politics, parliament and voting, as well as human rights, justice, media literacy, the law and the economy. Teaching is brought to life by drawing on real-life issues, current affairs, case studies, people and events in a variety of contexts, from local to global.

Established in 2002 as a stand-alone national curriculum subject for children from 11- to 16-years-old, it followed a 1998 report by the distinguished political philosopher, Bernard Crick. He recommended that the subject should concentrate on three things: social and moral responsibility, community involvement and, above all, political literacy.

In a speech to his union's annual conference in 2011, the president of the NAS/UWT teachers' union, John Rimmer, called for compulsory citizenship lessons for all pupils and explained why the new subject is so vital for maintaining a healthy democracy: 'It is important that pupils learn about the political system at school, rather than rely on the words of politicians after they've left.'[20]

With steadily declining electoral turnout and rising distrust of politicians, citizenship education (or democratic education, as it is also known) has never been more sorely needed. Sadly, it is not given either the respect or the resources it deserves. A 2021 report, based on a survey of 300 teachers in nearly 2,000 secondary schools, found that fewer than one in three establishments offered weekly lessons in politics or citizenship. Instead, many ran extra-curricular activities such as debating societies and mock elections, while one in five schools offered nothing at all. Provision was most systematic in independent schools and in state schools located in affluent areas.

One of the main reasons for the lack of citizenship education is a shortage of specialist teachers. The report, headed by James Weinberg of the University of Sheffield, paints a stark picture of under-recruitment: 'In the Department of Education 2019 school workforce survey, only 456 of 2,876 schools reported having a trained citizenship teacher. This is a shocking statistic, but possibly not surprising when you consider the historic training figures for this subject. Just 284 newly qualified teachers (NQTs) practised the subject in 2006 (against a target of 540). In 2010, only 220 citizenship teacher training places were available, and by 2017 the number of trainee citizenship teachers reportedly dropped to fewer than 50.'[21] The result is that citizenship is more often than not taught by non-specialists, more than half of whom are maths, science and PE teachers.

The report calls for more bursaries for trainee citizenship teachers. It also cites data which shows that parents in England rate Citizenship and Politics as equally important subjects for adult life in Britain as History, Geography, Chemistry and Physics (all of which are eligible for bursaries) and more important than Religion, Classics and Languages (which also qualify for financial support.)

Another problem is that, like arts subjects, citizenship is not considered as a core subject for the English Baccalaureate. A review of the national curriculum in 2013 created confusion, according to the Association for Citizenship Teaching (ACT), in evidence given to the House of Lords Select Committee on Citizenship and Civic Engagement. The ACT said the review 'led some schools to assume that the rumoured removal of the subject must have happened, and three years on, some still do not know that Citizenship remains in the National Curriculum or has a GCSE. Consequently, some schools have simply stopped teaching the subject.'[22]

Another factor has been the conversion of many schools previously run by local authorities into academies, which do not have to follow the national curriculum. Evidence suggests that many of them are taking advantage of their newfound freedom to drop citizenship from their timetables.

Regrettably, in today's Britain, whether you are taught how to be a good citizen seems to be a matter of luck, as Citizenship Foundation CEO Tom Franklin told a House of Lords Select Committee: 'Our current view is that citizenship education is withering on the vine at a time when it is needed more than ever. If we look at the polarisation of society and the undermining of the faith in democratic society, there is such a need for young people to develop the skills, knowledge and confidence, yet what is happening with citizenship education is that support for the subject has been dismantled. If we look at the fact that education regulators no longer focus on it; that there is not the support needed for teacher training ... Whether young people are receiving high-quality citizenship education is a lottery; it is by chance as to whether they are getting it in their school or not, which is a great shame.'[23]

* * *

David-Wallace Wells' terrifyingly titled book, *The Uninhabitable Earth—A Story Of The Future*, gives a sober analysis of the consequences of various degrees of global warming. The list of chapter headings tells you more than you probably care to know about what is going to happen to the human race if we don't try much harder to combat climate change: Heat Death, Hunger, Drowning, Wildfire, Dying Oceans, Unbreathable Air, Economic Collapse and Climate Conflict are just some of the lowlights of a truly apocalyptic future that awaits us if our efforts at remedial action continue at their current glacial pace (indeed before long there may well be more metaphorical glaciers than real ones).

Of all the threats covered in this chapter, climate change is the only one that threatens our very existence. If you're still not convinced, just try digesting one shocking morsel from Wallace-Wells' book: 'In 2018, in the journal *Nature Climate Change*, a team led by Drew Shindell tried to quantify the suffering that would be avoided if warming was kept to one-and-a-half degrees, rather than two degrees. Their answer: 150m more people would die from air pollution in a two-degree-warmer world than in a one-and-a-half degree warmer one. The figure of 150m is the equivalent of 25 Holocausts. It is more than twice the greatest death toll of any kind, including World War II. This is what is meant when climate change is called an 'existential crisis'—a drama we are now haphazardly improvising between two hellish poles, in which our best-case outcome is death and suffering at the scale of 25 Holocausts, and the worst-case outcome puts us on the brink of extinction.'[24]

A glimpse of what's in store for the UK can be seen in the fate of the village of Fairbourne on the North Wales coast. The local council has decided that rising sea levels mean that the village cannot be protected from flooding in the long term and must therefore be decommissioned by 2045 at the latest. Once the 850 residents are moved out of their homes, the whole village, including houses, shops, roads, sewers, gas pipes and electricity pylons, will be dismantled, turning the site back into a tidal salt marsh. With sea levels set to continue rising for centuries, the inhabitants of Fairbourne may be Britain's first climate refugees, but they certainly won't be the last.

The government's Committee on Climate Change (CCC) predicted in 2018 that by the 2080s, as many as 1.5m homes on the English coast will be at risk of flooding, with more than 100,000 at risk from coastal erosion. Jim Hall, the CCC report author and professor of climate and environmental risk at Oxford University, told *The Guardian:* 'The situation on the coast is a time bomb. About half the coast of England is protected with sea walls, promenades and other coastal defences. But many of these are reaching the end of their lives. It is just not going to be affordable to continue to protect large stretches of coastline.'[25]

The same process will also threaten London, according to Mark Maslin, the director of UCL's Environmental Institute. Citing predictions that sea levels will rise by 80cm by 2080, he told an audience at the Chatham House think-tank that, at any time after 2030, the Thames barrier could be breached, and London flooded. Professor Maslin warned that as many as 65 tube stations would be inundated, with the ensuing disruption to the capital city's economy a potential trigger for a global recession.[26]

Similar warnings have been issued by Climate Central, an independent organisation of leading scientists and journalists reporting the facts on the impact of climate change. Its interactive map of areas at high risk of flooding by 2050 includes large swathes of the capital's most expensive real estate, including Kensington and Chelsea, Pimlico, Fulham, Battersea and Wandsworth as well as the well-heeled suburbs of Chiswick, Richmond and Twickenham, further to the west.

Staff at the Natural History Museum in South Kensington are more worried about the UK's wildlife keeping its head above water than their flood-threatened stuffed exhibits. A study by the organisation's scientists found that almost half of the country's natural biodiversity has already disappeared, making Britain one of the world's worst nations for retaining its ecosystem's animals and plants. 'Britain has lost more of its natural biodiversity than almost anywhere else in western Europe, the most of all the G7 nations and more than many other nations such as China,' the museum's Professor Andy Purvis told *The Guardian*. 'It is very striking—and worrying'.[27] Species tottering at the edge of extinction include the pine marten, the Scottish wild cat, the natterjack toad and the turtle dove. Even the humble hedgehog is under threat. Climate change is accelerating the decline in biodiversity which up to now has been blamed mainly on urbanisation and the agricultural and industrial revolutions.

Given the high individual and collective costs involved, and the personal sacrifices that will have to be made, you might think that schools have already fully integrated climate change into their teaching programme. Yet the subject is hardly mentioned in England's national curriculum. For example, the word 'climate' features only twice in the science curriculum (in Key Stage Three for 12 to 14-year-olds and again in Key Stage Four for 15- and 16-year-olds). For children between the ages of five and 11, it is completely absent from science lessons.

Environmental campaigners say this softly-softly approach to teaching climate change merits a triple-underlined 'must try harder' verdict. Professor Andrew Charlton-Perez of Reading University thinks there is considerable scope for including climate change in a much wider range of subjects: 'For example, food technology pupils could learn about low-carbon foods and cooking techniques. English pupils could study methods of communicating risk. Business lessons could feature work on estimating and preparing for commercial risks associated with extreme weather.'[28] UN accredited climate change teacher, Meryl Batchelder, agrees that climate change education should be a thread running through all subjects, not just science (which she teaches) and geography: 'From the food miles of the ingredients we cook in food technology, to debates on humanitarian issues such as mass migration in religious education, we need a green curriculum that starts in the early years and extends through all key stages.'[29]

According to a recent survey of 4,690 teachers in England, two-thirds said that, in their subject area, climate change was not taught in a meaningful or relevant way, while seven out of 10 said they had not been adequately trained to teach it. Science, Geography and PSHE (Personal, Social, Health and Economic education) were the lessons most likely to mention climate change (though geography, the subject with the most climate-related content, is not compulsory at GCSE level).

Teach the Future, the campaign group that commissioned the research, is calling for more systematic teaching of climate change throughout the curriculum, with more resources devoted to compulsory teacher training in the subject. It also wants more emphasis on green skills in vocational education (for example retraining plumbers to install solar panels, batteries and heat pumps instead of gas fired boilers). Finally, it calls for investment to make all educational buildings, many of which are currently environmentally wasteful and powered by fossil fuels, fully net-zero compliant by 2030.[30]

At the 2021 Cop26 summit in Glasgow, the government pledged to 'put climate change at the heart of education.' An official predicted that: 'By 2023 all teachers in all phases and subjects will have access to high-quality curriculum resources,' with children given the opportunity for 'hands-on experience of understanding, nurturing and protecting the biodiversity around them.'[31] Those are words that could be music to the ears of climate campaigners if they are backed up by action.

* * *

At the time of writing, our education system is in turmoil, still reeling from the Covid lockdowns and embroiled in long-running industrial action over teachers' pay and conditions, and controversy surrounding Ofsted school inspections. Despite the discouraging context, we should not be distracted from the need to radically reform the school curriculum to address the major challenges that threaten our democracy and economy. We need a modern-day Sir Billy Biscuit, an influential figure with the foresight to value and promote the four Cs!

CONCLUSION

Sinking, giggling, into the sea?

I'm a big fan of the series of jokes about light bulbs. There are many variants, all revolving around the simple task of replacing a defective light bulb. So, for example, there's 'How many climate change sceptics does it take to screw in a light bulb? Answer: none, because it's too early to tell if the lightbulb really needs changing.' Or how about 'How many Manchester United fans does it take to screw in a light bulb? Answer: 10—one to screw in the light bulb and the other nine to reminisce about how good the old one was.' But my all-time favourite light bulb joke is: 'How many psychiatrists does it take to screw in a light bulb? Answer: only one, but the light bulb must want to be changed.'

For me, the significance of this punchline extends far beyond humour. It can apply to many situations in our everyday lives, but it is also highly relevant to the UK in its current predicament. Because, no matter how many sensible reforms are proposed in this book, they will never happen unless the country accepts that radical change is necessary. In this concluding chapter, I will examine the paradox of why the UK should be so resistant to fundamental reform in the fields of democracy and education, when it has undergone such huge economic and social changes in the past half century. But first, let's remind ourselves of why reform is so badly needed.

In the world of human rights, there's an interesting concept called intersectionality. It describes how one person can suffer from discrimination on several separate levels. For example, a woman can be discriminated against because of her gender. If she has a disability, that will likely result in her being discriminated against in a different way. If she's a black woman with a disability, discrimination will come at her from three directions, and if she's a gay, black, disabled woman, she may experience discrimination from four separate sources. This concept can also be applied to the UK because, as a nation, we are facing tough challenges on multiple fronts.

The first is that more and more of us are becoming poor. According to the Joseph Rowntree Trust, more than one in five UK citizens are now living in poverty.[1] Of these 14.5m people, more than 8m are working-age adults, 4.3m are children, and 2.1m are pensioners. Most worryingly, child poverty is on the increase—nearly one in three children (31 per cent) are living in poverty, rising to one in two in single-parent homes, compared with 'only' one in four in families consisting of couples. Among pensioners, nearly one in five are poor, compared with one in eight a decade ago. In the year from 2008-9, only 26,000 people used UK food banks. By 2021-22 this number had increased to 2.1m. Surging inflation, especially for food and energy, is likely to tip even more people into poverty.

The UK is now the most unequal country in Europe, except for Bulgaria. Yet according to the International Monetary Fund, in 2023, we were still the sixth largest economy in the world (by nominal Gross Domestic Product), behind the USA, China, Japan, Germany and India and ahead of France and Italy. That both these facts can be true isn't just a national scandal, it's also a matter of life and death, as poverty has significant health impacts. Writing in *The Guardian*, Professor Michael Marmot, a specialist in epidemiology and public health at University College London, spelled out the risks: 'In the decade before the pandemic, improvement in health in the UK slowed dramatically, inequalities increased, and health for the poorest people got worse. This was all amplified by the pandemic. Unless we deal with the inability of people to meet their basic needs, by adequate income and services, we are in danger of inflicting a humanitarian calamity in one of the richest countries in the world.'[2]

Poverty and inequality are the main reasons why the UK has, for decades, been hurtling down the global rankings of life expectancy. New research published in the *Journal of the Royal Society of Medicine* reveals that in 1952, when Queen Elizabeth came to the throne, the UK had one of the longest life expectancies in the world, ranking seventh globally behind countries like Norway, Sweden and Denmark. But, by 2021, the UK was ranked 29th. People in Britain are on average still living longer lives than they were in 1952, but 28 countries are extending their citizens' life expectancies for longer than the UK. The researchers point to income inequalities, which rose greatly in the UK during and after the 1980s.

Professor Martin McKee of the London School of Hygiene and Tropical Medicine explained: 'One reason why the overall increase in life expectancy has been so sluggish in the UK is that, in recent years, it has fallen for poorer (socio-economic) groups.' According to another of the researchers, Dr Lucinda Hiam of Oxford University: 'A relative worsening of population health is evidence that all is not well. It has historically been an early sign of severe political and economic problems. This new analysis suggests that the problems the UK faces are deep seated and raises serious questions about the path that this country is following.'[3]

Of course, it doesn't help that the British have the worst access to medical care in Europe. According to *The Financial*

Times' data analysis expert, John Burn-Murdoch, in the year to November 2022, 'one in six UK adults has had a pressing need for medical examination or treatment and been unable to get access, with almost half of these cases due to the length of waiting lists. This is the highest figure out of 36 European countries and almost triple the EU average.'[4]

After poverty, the second major challenge facing the UK is how to improve our lacklustre industrial productivity. Unless we can make more with less, our economy will stagnate, and without growth we cannot increase spending on public services such as the NHS and education. Sadly, we have not advanced much on this front in the four decades since Margaret Thatcher came to power. In 1980, we came fifth from bottom for output per hour, compared with 15 of our European neighbours. By 2019, we had fallen to fourth from bottom, ahead only of Greece, Portugal and Spain. France and America are both around 20 per cent more productive than the UK, while Germany is 10 per cent more output efficient. The causes of our lagging productivity are easy to identify but notoriously hard to tackle. The UK invests 10 per cent of its GDP in new machinery, factories, information technology, logistics and research and development. The French, Germans and Americans plough an annual 13 per cent into these same factors of production. It may not seem like a great deal, but it represents nearly a third more annual investment than Britain is currently making.

As well as under investment, Britain also suffers from generally poor management. Part of the problem lies with too many family-run firms. Business journalist Jonty Bloom explained in *The New European* how this is sometimes referred to as the Tokyo Olympics problem. 'Would you have picked the British squad for last year's Tokyo Olympics by just selecting the grandchildren of the team that went to Tokyo in 1964? Obviously not, but that is what you are doing when you appoint your children to the board. In Germany, where there are many highly successful family-owned firms, they are far more likely to be professionally run.'[5] Add to this that many of the brightest British graduates shun the world of management in favour of a better-paid career in finance, medicine or the law, and it's not hard to see why many European countries have higher quality managers than we do.

On top of rising poverty and sluggish to non-existent productivity growth, there's also the problem of the UK's fast ageing population. By 2030 there will be 4.4m people over the age of 80, compared with 3m now. The state spends about £20,000 per year on each child of school age, but double that amount on every person in their late 80s, much of it on healthcare. By 2024, the NHS will consume 44 per cent of the state's day-to-day spending compared with around 27 per cent in 2000. If spending remains constant in real terms, that means the rest of the state's provisions—education, defence, social security and so on—will have to shrink.

According to *The Economist*, the result will be shrinkflation. Like a well-known brand of chocolate bar that gets smaller each year, taxpayers will get less and less for their money. 'British voters are often said to want American taxes and a European welfare state. Instead, they face paying European taxes for services as skimpy as those in America.'[6]

Then there's Brexit. Whether you voted Leave or Remain, or, like me, you didn't get a vote at all, there's no denying that making it harder to do business with the world's biggest trading bloc was always going to hurt the UK economy. From the long queues of lorries at Dover to the £13bn a year in extra form filling costs for importers and exporters, Brexit is a heavy drag on trade with our nearest neighbours. The Office of Budget Responsibility has estimated the annual long-term cost of Brexit at four per cent of GDP, or about £32bn a year, based on 2021 figures.

In 2019, Honda announced it was closing its factory in Swindon after 35 years, with the loss of 3,000 jobs. Professor Andrew Graves, a motor industry expert from the University of Bath, told the BBC: 'The Swindon factory was world-class, but, because we chose to pull out of Europe, which was the most important market to Honda, they chose to stick with America and Japan. Brexit was the straw that broke the camel's back.'[7] In the 1990s the UK was dubbed 'The Japanese aircraft carrier floating off the coast of Europe' by an envious French car industry executive. But if the Honda decision is anything to go by, the Japanese car makers are now thinking seriously about jumping ship.

Meanwhile, others are choosing not to get on board in the first place. The world's richest man, Elon Musk, dropped his plan to build Tesla's European Gigafactory in Somerset, and instead spent $5.5bn on building the plant near Berlin, where it now employs 10,000 people. Asked about his change of mind, he cited Brexit uncertainty as the main reason.

At the time of writing, the UK has not yet re-joined the EU's Horizon Europe programme for funding cross-border scientific cooperation. According to the Royal Society, which represents Britain's leading scientists: 'The UK's participation in EU Framework Programmes for research and innovation has been crucial to growth and global influence and brought significant benefits to people living in the UK. Pursuing association to the next Framework Programme, Horizon Europe, is critical to maintaining our place at the heart of international science.'[8] As we saw in chapter 10, cutting-edge scientific research and innovation is the key to Britain's future prosperity.

The challenges facing the UK are indeed formidable. Tackling them would have been much easier had we put money away for a rainy day. In the 1980s, the British government was earning £18bn a year from taxing North Sea oil and gas revenues. But, instead of saving some of the income from this fossil-fuelled bonanza for future generations, the windfall was used to keep taxes low and the pound high. Conservative grandee Michael Heseltine says he would have preferred the money to have been invested in a sovereign wealth fund, a state-owned financial instrument aimed at securing long-term benefits for the nation's citizenry.

Norway's Oil Fund is now worth more than $1tr, owns one per cent of the world's stocks and shares and has made paper millionaires of each and every one of the country's 3m citizens. While Norway is now the world's second wealthiest country (after Luxembourg), the UK languishes in 20th place, with a GDP per capita only half the size of its North Sea neighbour.

Also, unlike Norway and most other European democracies, in the 1980s, the UK sold off its nationalised industries, raising billions of pounds for the Exchequer but losing control of key utilities such as water, gas, electricity and telecoms. Ironically, many are now in the hands of state-owned enterprises from other countries. For example, Britain's energy market is dominated by foreign giants such as France's EDF, Germany's Innogy and E.ON and Spain's Iberdrola. Major rail franchises are run by the likes of Deutsche Bahn (Germany), Abelllio (Netherlands) and Keolis (France). Thames Water is owned by an international consortium while Wessex Water belongs to Malaysia's YTL Power International. A consortium of overseas investors owns Heathrow Airport Holdings, while Gatwick belongs to

Global Infrastructure Partners, an international investment fund. The country's ports are mostly in foreign hands while the flagship P&O shipping and passenger line is owned by the Dubai-based port operator DP World. As Nick Pearce wrote in *The New Statesman:* 'Ironically, it is those who now argue most vociferously for *taking back control* that did the most to give it away in the first place.'[9]

The sale of council housing to tenants under the Right to Buy legislation raised similarly vast sums for the government, but many former local authority properties ended up being transferred by their new owners to landlords, who rented them out at market rates. So instead of achieving the original aim of extending home ownership, in many cases the operation simply transferred properties from the public rental sector to its private equivalent. As with North Sea oil, there was no attempt to use the receipts from privatisation and council house sales for long-term investment in the country's future.

Conservative statesman Harold MacMillan was a trenchant critic of privatisation. He is often mis-quoted as having described it as a policy of 'selling off the family silver.' What he really said was rather more subtle, but with the same message: 'First of all the Georgian silver goes, and then all that nice furniture in the saloon. Then the Canalettos go.' Now that all the Canalettos have been sold off, Britain finds itself in a tight spot, facing the headwinds of a full-scale European war, fallout from Brexit and Covid, not to mention the twin long-term threats of climate change and job-destroying technology.

So what shape is our venerable democratic infrastructure in, to help us meet these enormous challenges? In the age of gene editing, the metaverse and Abba avatars we have a political system inherited from the age of the horse and cart. If it were a ship, it would be declared unseaworthy. If it were a car, it would fail its MOT (Ministry of Transport) Test. If it were a computer, it would be thrown into a skip. Of all European countries, only the UK is happy to put its faith in a clapped-out political system at least half a century past its sell-by date. To recycle a Conservative slogan from the 1979 election campaign: "Britain isn't working!"

The question is, are we going to do anything about it? Or do we prefer to sit on our hands and passively accept what satirist Peter Cook described as the danger of the country 'sinking, giggling, into the sea'? (The giggling presumably sustained by those side-splittingly amusing PMQs exchanges and the hilarious headlines served up by the likes of *The Sun* and *The Daily Star*).

The paradox is that in almost every other sector of national life, the UK has changed beyond recognition since 1960, the year I was born. During these six decades, we have lost what remained of our empire, replaced a manufacturing economy with one focused mainly on services, seen a huge decline in the power of trades unions, made big strides in tackling discrimination on grounds of race, gender and sexual orientation, abolished fox hunting, allowed Sunday shopping, achieved peace in Northern Ireland while fighting wars in the Falklands, Iraq and Afghanistan, and opened up higher education to many more students. We have become a more tolerant nation but also a much less equal one, with the chasm between rich and poor widening so much that we now have more in common with America's vast social divides than with our more socially cohesive European neighbours.

When it comes to democratic progress there is much less to report. The main developments have been the introduction of directly elected metropolitan mayors responsible for the strategic development of a city region (notable examples being Manchester's Andy Burnham and his Birmingham counterpart, Andy Street) and devolution in Northern Ireland, Scotland, and Wales. The Welsh Senedd and the Scottish Parliament have been particularly instructive in demonstrating how national politics could benefit from a constitutional upgrade. Cardiff and Edinburgh both have modern parliament buildings with circular debating chambers, where the number of seats miraculously matches the number of politicians.

Needless to say, these functional surroundings, which bear no architectural resemblance to either public schools or the Oxford Union debating society, discourage the kind of immature barracking that brings PMQs into such disrepute at Westminster. Another positive feature is that the devolved assemblies use more representative voting systems than Westminster. These not only yield fairer election results but also encourage European-style cross-party cooperation.

In Wales, the ruling coalition is between Labour and Plaid Cymru, the Welsh nationalist party. In Scotland, the Scottish National Party shares power with the Greens. But perhaps the most interesting aspect of these devolved assemblies is the kind of leader they have produced. Both the current Welsh First Minister Mark Drakeford and his former Scottish counterpart Nichola Sturgeon come from modest backgrounds. They did not go to private schools, let alone Eton, and neither attended an Oxbridge college. Both had real jobs before entering politics: Drakeford was a probation officer while Sturgeon was a solicitor. Their calm handling of the Covid crisis was evidence that elite public schools and Oxbridge do not have a monopoly on leadership talent.

These advances in devolution apart, there remains stubborn resistance to more fundamental institutional reform at national level. A proposal to introduce a fairer voting system for national parliamentary elections was heavily defeated in a referendum held in 2011, while there seems to be scant political will to contemplate further reform of the House of Lords, let alone drafting a codified constitution. There is even less appetite for tackling the injustices and shortcomings of the education system, which would do so much to support and improve our democracy and economy. So, what accounts for this apathy, or more accurately antipathy, to bringing our democratic and educational infrastructure up to scratch? Or to put it a different way, why are we so addicted to our traditional way of doing things?

Being an island has much to do with it. Had we been invaded by, for example, Napoleon, our aristocratic elites—along with their privileges and traditions—would have been swept away, and in time we would have rebuilt our institutions along modern lines. More fundamentally, living under foreign dictatorial rule would have brought us into line with our European neighbours, most of whom have been occupied by external powers, in some cases on multiple occasions. Undoubtedly, occupation would have nipped British exceptionalism in the bud.

None of this is to have wished national humiliation on Britain, but there are many who believe that the pain of a one-time military defeat would have brought long-term gains in terms of restructuring British society for the better. Instead, argued Simon Kuper in *The Financial Times*, excessive stability has bred complacency: 'Contrast all this (upheavals in 20th century France) with England, which has gone more than 300 years without revolution, civil war or serious invasion. Inevitably the English have grown complacent about potential disasters ... The most complacent English caste of all is the ruling class—which is understandable, given that it hasn't been replaced in centuries. If your life passage takes you from medieval rural home to medieval boarding school to medieval Oxbridge college and finally to medieval parliament, you naturally end up thinking 'what could possibly go wrong?'[10]

A Dutch journalist who lived for many years in the UK goes even further. In an article for *Prospect* magazine entitled, *England, You Lot Need A Good Occupation!*, Joris Luyendijk wrote: 'Here lies the root cause of so many of this country's problems; for it is the reason why you're still stuck with your old elites. These elites will either shaft you, causing great bitterness, or they manage to co-opt you, leading to feelings of guilt (*The Guardian*) or contempt (*The Daily Telegraph*). Stop all this nonsense about a global role or race and put your energy into giving your people a decent life, while being good neighbours to the countries around you.'[11]

Never having refreshed our elites also explains our addiction to tradition, symbolised most recently by Queen Elizabeth's funeral and the new King's coronation. All harmless fun as far as democracy is concerned, unless of course you happen to be a republican. But the same cannot be said of traditions that involve the democratic process. The state opening of parliament is a good example. It involves an official called Black Rod getting ritually refused entry to the House of Commons before eventually leading the assembled MPs to the House of Lords, where the King makes a speech from a throne, outlining the government's new legislative programme. What's the difference between this ceremony and Trooping The Colour? Isn't it equally harmless?

The answer is that, if we moved our parliament to a modern building, say in Birmingham or Manchester, it would be inconceivable that the Black Rod show, complete with medieval garb and throne, could be transplanted into the new theatre of democracy. And just as there are many people who still yearn for shillings and farthings, pounds and ounces, there would be those who would baulk at moving our parliament into a state-of-the-art building, if that meant ditching a meaningless centuries old tradition. So Black Rod turns out to be a red line against modernisation. Many MPs, as well as members of the public, would rather spend billions on restoring a building with a debating chamber designed to encourage confrontation at the expense of compromise, than investing a small fraction of those huge sums on a purpose-built parliament equipped with all mod cons.

Which brings us to the widest roadblock to reforming our country's institutions. The class system is the biggest elephant in the room. Nobody wants to talk about class, because it's embarrassing, like revealing to other people how much you earn. This self-imposed radio silence makes invisible discrimination easy to ignore. Those who escape from the working class are usually keener on fitting into their new social milieu than campaigning for better mobility opportunities for people from their own background. Those born into the middle and upper classes have no reason to make it harder for their own children to succeed in life by reducing their privileges. This explains why there are no job adverts with sentences like, 'We accept applicants from working-class backgrounds,' let alone, 'We are an equal opportunities employer. Preference will be given to working-class applicants.'

When I worked at the BBC in the 1980s, there was a drive to recruit more journalists from ethnic minority backgrounds. The initiative succeeded in creating a more diverse newsroom, but it did nothing for social mobility, because most of those appointed came from elite backgrounds. Here are some of the best-known names from that period, together with the private schools they attended: Mishal Husain (Cobham Hall School, £24,000 a year for day pupils), Rageh Omaar (the Dragon School, Oxford, £24,000) Matthew Amroliwala (King's Ely, £25,000) and Reeta Chakrabarti (King Edward VI High School for Girls, Birmingham, £15,000). A recent survey by *UK Press Gazette* revealed that 80 per cent of journalists now come from upper-class backgrounds. Only two per cent had a parent from the lowest two occupational groups.[12] But don't expect the BBC, or any other media employer, to launch a working-class recruitment drive anytime soon.

When the Vice-Chancellor of Cambridge University told a journalist from *The Times* that his university would be deliberately accepting fewer candidates from private schools, the story made the front page of the newspaper, no doubt causing Disgusted of Tunbridge Wells and countless other disgruntled Home Counties-based readers to choke on their cornflakes. This gives us a clue as to why there is no appetite in the UK for reforming our institutions—it might upset the class-privilege apple cart that has, for centuries, kept the lower orders firmly in their place.

In her book. *There is Nothing For You Here,* Fiona Hill, a former top Russia adviser to three American presidents, recounts her journey from a working-class home in Bishop Auckland, County Durham, to St Andrews University, Harvard, and the White House. She recalls being cynically quizzed by middle-class children from other schools about her social origins:

'In our first encounters, many of them grilled me with a set of three questions that would follow me from my childhood to adulthood, all in the following order:

1. 'So, where are you from, then?'
2. 'What does your father do?' (there was no follow-up about my mother), and
3. 'What school did you go to?'

'The questions seemed innocent at first, yet I quickly realised that they were anything but. They were not the opener for a "Let's get to know each other" conversation. This was a highly determinative trifecta of questions—the beginning of a socioeconomic class-sorting exercise. Depending on how you answered, you could be either accepted or written off.'[13]

Unlike Fiona Hill, Dutch journalist Joris Luyendijk witnessed the snobbery and rank unfairness of the British class system from the outside: 'It is quite ironic that a nation that gave the world the term "fair play" sees the fact that rich children receive a better education than poor ones as a perfectly natural thing. Nor do I blame working-class people for seething at a system where by the time you are 11 the die is cast, and where—to add insult to injury—you are constantly told that this is a meritocracy where all that counts is hard work and being aspirational ... George Orwell is still correct: England is a family with the wrong members in charge.'[14]

Tackling Britain's class problem is not just a question of social justice, it's ultimately a question of national economic survival. For any post-industrial country to thrive, it must make the most of its population's potential, and that includes the working class. But the knowledge economy won't bear fruit if Britain continues to spaff away its human talent. Miner's daughter Fiona Hill nailed it in the final chapter of her book, *'There is Nothing For You Here'*—just substitute 'Britain' for 'the United States' and you have a perfect analysis of our national malaise:

'In many respects, the United States has wasted human

capital on an enormous scale over the last 40 years by constraining social mobility for millions of people. Ultimately, the United States is only as good as the quality of its population, in terms of its general health and well-being and educational attainment. People, individually and collectively, form the core of America's institutions and drive innovation, yet too often they are an afterthought in our national conversations and our leaders' policy decisions."[15]

If we want to maximise the potential of UK plc's human capital, it's not enough to change our leaders once every five years—we have to make radical changes to our manifestly dysfunctional system. We need to follow the example of other countries that have taken bold steps to modernise their political infrastructure.

In 2020, Italians voted by an overwhelming majority to reduce the size of their two-chamber parliament from 945 to 600, reducing it to less than half the size of the British equivalent. The following year, President Macron abolished ENA (*Ecole National d'Administration*), the training school for the French elite set up by President de Gaulle at the end of the Second World War. Increasingly viewed as a symbol of entrenched privilege, it was the equivalent of the British government shutting down Eton and Oxbridge in one fell swoop. Perhaps the most relevant example for the UK is the use of citizens' assemblies in the Irish Republic to discuss the controversial issues of abortion and gay marriage. The deliberations led to referendums which legalised both activities.

If there's one lesson in this book, it's that who's in charge is not as important as the system they are in charge of. Allow me to use a maritime example to illustrate the source of our seafaring nation's plight. The story of *The RMS Titanic* is recounted as a disaster not because it hit an iceberg and sank, but because there were not enough lifeboats to save everyone. The reason for the shortage was that successive parliaments had vetoed legislation to force ship owners to carry an adequate number of lifeboats. Britain's recurrent political psychodramas are the equivalent of reconfiguring the deck chairs on that ill-fated vessel. We need to look beyond the personalities of the captain and crew and examine the weak points of our ship before taking steps to strengthen it against future shocks. My personal first priority would be to scrap our unfair and unrepresentative electoral system.

Like global Britain, *The Titanic* had world-beating aspirations, but it ended up at the bottom of the Atlantic. If we want to avoid a similar fate, we have to take urgent action because time is running out and water is running in. We have to choose between transforming ourselves into a modern democracy or retaining our debilitating system of tradition, class and privilege. Are we going to sink, giggling, into the sea—or rise from our sick bed? Historian Thomas

Otte paints a bleak picture of the country's future if our leaders choose the former option:

'As for Britain's final destiny, she may well find herself restored to the position of Elizabethan England: a country on the north-western periphery of European politics, culturally vibrant no doubt, but of marginal significance politically, dependent for its precarious prosperity on foreign trade, though highly suspicious of foreign countries and internally deeply divided. A country of a little over 65m trying to strike out on its own will have to live on its wits and rely on a good deal of that rarest of political commodities, good luck.'[16]

Finally, let's return to the subject of jokes involving light bulbs. Here's mine: 'How many British politicians does it take to change a light bulb? Answer: None, because they all agree that the broken light bulb is still working wonderfully well.'

If that turns out to be true, then the joke really will be on all of us. And that's no laughing matter.

NOTES

INTRODUCTION

1. John Burns-Murdoch, 'Britain and the US are poor societies with some very rich people' the Financial Times, 16 September 2022.
2. Said by Rhodes to Lord Grey, 'The Life and Times of the Right Honourable Cecil John Rhodes 1853-1902, Volume 2', by Lewis Mitchell, Franklin Classics Trade Press, 2018. p.178.
3. Fiona Harvey, 'England 'failing to invest in water networks to avoid future droughts', Guardian, 15 August 2022.
4. Martin Fletcher, 'Britain's painful decline since the 2012 London Olympics', New Statesman, 8 August 2022.

CHAPTER ONE

1. Sir Winston Churchill in his speech during a debate on the House of Commons Rebuilding, October 28, 1943, Hansard vol 393 cc 403.
2. Ian Dunt speaking on the podcast 'Oh God, What Now?' on 6 July 2022.
3. Max Cohen de Lara and David Mulder van der Vegt, 'Parliament', XML Partners, Amsterdam 2016.
4. Interview by the author with Professor Matthew Flinders, 2 July 2019.
5. Hansard, Vol. 626, 27 June 2017, 4.34pm, Maiden speech of Laura Pidcock MP.
6. 'Restoration and Renewal Programme: Strategic Review'. Houses of Parliament Restoration and Renewal (March 2021).
7. Chris Bowlby: 'Parliament - A Building Catastrophe?', BBC Radio 4, 23 October 2017. See also https://www.bbc.com/news/uk-politics-41650215.
8. 1st Report – Restoration and Renewal Committee of the Palace of Westminster, 8 September 2016 https://committees.parliament.uk/work/5893/restoration-and-renewal-of-the-palace-of-westminster-consultation.
9. Richard Rogers, 'The Welsh Assembly', in Design Commission, Designing Democracy (London, Policy Connect, 2015), pp.13-14.
10. John Kampfner, 'Why the Germans Do it Better: Notes from a Grown Up Country', Atlantic Books, London, 2020, p.72.

11. From the same source, p.74.
12. Interview by the author with Professor Matthew Flinders, 2 July 2019.

CHAPTER TWO

1. Tom Calver and Rosamund Urwin, 'House of Lords expenses spiral out of control', Sunday Times, 23 February 2020.
2. Brexit and Exit - Episode 3 of BBC television documentary series 'Meet the Lords', first broadcast on 13 March 2017.
3. Simon Walters and Brendan Carlin, 'House of Frauds: Cheating peers claim £300 for just a few minutes' work as their taxis run outside, says 'Baroness of Excess', Mail on Sunday, 4 February 2017.
4. Andrew Pierce 'Reforming the Lords through emasculation', Daily Telegraph, 10 March 2007.
5. Rebel Lords - Episode 2 of BBC documentary series 'Meet the Lords', first broadcast on 6 March 2017.
6. Marie Woolf, 'Earl of Limerick turns poetic in bid for Lords seat', Times, 8 November 2015.
7. Mary Wakefield, 'Tony Benn 1924-2014: A politician who actually believed in people', Spectator, 14 March 2014.
8. Anne Perkins, 'The People's Peers: seven knights, a lord's wife and three professors', Guardian, 27 April 2001.
9. Simon Murphy and Jim Waterson, 'Evgeny Lebedev, Jo Johnson and Ian Botham among 36 peerage nominations', Guardian, 31 July 2020.
10. Lord Speaker statement on new appointments, 31 July 2020. https://www.parliament.uk/business/news/2020/july/lord-speaker-comments-on-new-appo.
11. Jim Pickard and Laura Hughes, 'Latest Lords appointment raises questions over party donors', Financial Times, 1 August 2020.
12. UK Parliament, Parliamentary archives, Lloyd George papers.
13. Patrick Wintour, 'Lords reform committee divided over key issues', Guardian, 23 April 2012.
14. Meg Russell and Tom Semlyen, 'Enough is Enough - Regulating Prime Ministerial Appointments to the Lords', p.55.
15. Roger Parry, 'Renovation - Rebuilding UK Politics', 2020, pp.63-67.
16. Labour Party plans to reform the House of Lords: 'A New Britain: Renewing our democracy and Rebuilding our Economy', 5 December 2022, pp.133-142.
17. Andrew Rawnsley, 'The House of Lords is absurd because it suits MPs to keep it that way', Observer, 9 August 2020.
18. From the same source.
19. Anthony Barnett and Peter Carty, 'The Athenian Option: Radical Reform for the House of Lords', Anthony Barnett and Peter Carty, Imprint Academic, 2008 (second edition).
20. Richard Askwith, 'Remaking Parliament for the Populist Age', Biteback Publishing, 2018, p.107.

CHAPTER THREE

1. Jonathan Lis, 'The entire constitution is now at stake', Byline Times, 14 April 2022.
2. Hannah White, 'What Boris Johnson taught us about the UK constitution', Prospect magazine, 17 August 2022.
3. Overheard when the Queen attended a seminar about the British Constitution at Queen Mary and Westfield College, University of London, 1992.
4. Tom Bingham, 'Lives in the Law', Oxford University Press, 2011, chapter 6.

5. Linda Colley, 'Why Britain needs a written constitution', Financial Times, 12 March 2021
6. Sidney Low, 'The Governance of England', Fisher Unwin, London, 1904, p.12.
7. Alexander Runswick, 'A UK constitution for the people, by the people', Financial Times, 4 April 2019.
8. Lecture of Lord Hailsham and Richard Dimbleby, BBC radio, 14 October 1976.
9. Sionaidh Douglas-Scott, 'The case against parliamentary sovereignty', Prospect magazine, 30 December 2021.
10. A.V. Dicey 1885.
11. Graham Allen MP, 'The last Prime Minister', Imprint Academic, 2003, p.12.
12. Adam Tucker, 'The Queen has more power over British laws than we ever thought', Guardian, 8 February 2021.
13. Norman Baker, 'Queen's consent is a constitutional outrage - parliament must abolish it', Guardian, 10 February 2021.
14. Peter Hennessy, 'Harvesting the Cupboards': Why Britain has produced No Administrative Theory or Ideology in the Twentieth Century'. Transactions of the Royal Historical Society, 4 (1994), p.205.
15. Andrew Blick and Peter Hennessy, 'The Bonfire of the Decencies: Repairing and Restoring the British Constitution', Haus Publishing, 2022, p.145.
16. Linda Colley, 'Why Britain needs a written constitution', Financial Times, 12 March 2021.

CHAPTER FOUR

1. 'End booing and jeering in parliament as poll shows voters lose respect for politicians when watching debates' iNews, 6 June 2022.
2. Paul Taylor, 'Britain's culture of confrontation', Politico, 5 April 2019.
3. Ayesha Hazarika & Tom Hamilton, 'Punch and Judy Politics - an Insider's Guide to Prime Minister's Questions', Biteback Publishing, 2019, p.30.
4. Ayesha Hazarika & Tom Hamilton, 'Punch and Judy Politics - an Insider's Guide to Prime Minister's Questions', p.44.
5. Nigel Morris, 'Ed Miliband and Nick Clegg back John Bercow's plans to reform PMQs - but Conservative backbenchers resist', Independent, 18 February 2014.
6. Peter Riddell, Institute for Government, 22 July 2011. https://www.instituteforgovernment.org.uk/article/comment/prime-ministers-questions.
7. Alex Marshall, 'A Show That Laughs at Boris Johnson, and May Have Aided His Rise', New York Times, 29 October 2019.
8. Peter Chappell, 'What Keir Starmer can learn from the failure of Jo Swinson', Prospect magazine, 14 February 2020.
9. Philip Oltermann, 'Germans look to liven up Berlin politics with a bit of Westminster knockabout', Guardian, 25 September 2014.
10. Richard Power Sayeed, 'The "Zoom Parliament" could inspire a more democratic House of Commons', Guardian, 26 April 2020.
11. Hannah White, 'The ludicrous decision to scrap the virtual parliament', Prospect magazine, 4 June 2020.

CHAPTER FIVE

1. Tim Farron, speech at the Liberal Democrats' YES! to Fairer Votes campaign launch, Manchester, 18 March 2011.
2. Juliette Jowit, 'The tragedy of the Commons: MP's are too busy to do their jobs', Guardian, 27 May 2015.
3. Interview by the author on 27 January 2020.

4. 'The governance of Britain: review of voting systems in the UK since 1997' published by the Ministry of Justice in January 2008, p.139, section 7.15.
5. The BBC News website explains how the STV voting system works: https://www.bbc.co.uk/news/uk-northern-ireland-61022550.
6. Nigel Farage, 'A new electoral system would save Britain from socialist decline', Daily Telegraph, 29 June 2022.
7. Referenced in a letter from David Healey of Sutton Coldfield to the Financial Times, published on 17 December 2019: 'Workings of UK electoral system are a scandal'.
8. Robert Cooper, 'The Ambassadors: Thinking about Diplomacy from Machiavelli to Modern Times', Weidenfeld & Nicholson, February 2021, p.491.

CHAPTER SIX

1. Simon Parker, 'Taking Power Back - Putting People in Charge of Politics', Policy Press, 2015, p.4.
2. Anthony King and Ivor Crewe, 'The Blunders of our Governments', OneWorld Publications, 2013, p. ix.
3. 'Why Britain is more geographically unequal than any other rich country', Economist, 20 July 2020.
4. Simon Parker, 'Taking Power Back - Putting People in Charge of Politics', Policy Press, 2015, p.34.
5. James Pickford, 'Recovery likely to widen the wealth gap between London and regions', Financial Times, 19 February 2019.
6. Janan Ganesh, 'Europe could see more Catalonias', Financial Times, 23 October 2017.
7. Speaking on the UK in a Changing Europe's 'Brexit Breakdown' podcast on 29 May 2020.
8. Judith Staines, 'Council builds £1bn property portfolio to sidestep UK austerity', Financial Times, 17 February 2019.
9. Ed Davey, 'Barnet and Lambeth turn to Easyjet and John Lewis', BBC News London, 29 April 2010.
10. From the same source.
11. From the same source.
12. Peter Hetherington, 'Local elections: Biggest issue facing councils isn't even up for debate', New European, 2 May 2018.
13. Tom Crewe, 'The Strange Death of Municipal England', London Review of Books, 15 December 2016.
14. John Harris, 'Levelling up? Most of the UK is still in the grip of austerity', Guardian, 28 February 2021.
15. Julian Ralph, 'The Best Government City in the World', Harpers New Monthly Magazine, 1890.
16. Walsall MP John McShane speaking in House of Commons debate on Local Authorities (Enabling) Bill, 14 February 1930, Hansard volume 235.
17. Steve Leach, John Stewart and George Jones, 'Centralisation, Devolution and the Future of Local Government in England'. Routledge, 2018, p.134.
18. Interview with the author on 21 December 2020.
19. Interview with the author on 10 December 2020.
20. John Harris, 'The pandemic has exposed the failings of Britain's centralised state', Guardian, 25 May 2020.

CHAPTER SEVEN

1. 'The Germans' episode of Fawlty Towers was aired for the first time on 24 October 1975

2. Gideon Rachman, 'Brexit reinforces Britain's imperial amnesia', Financial Times, 27 March 2017.
3. Benjamin Mueller, 'There Is, in Britain, a Very Big Silence around Race', New York Times, 11 March 2021.
4. Sathnam Sanghera, 'Empireland - how imperialism has shaped modern Britain', 2021, Viking Penguin, p.152.
5. Maya Oppenheim, 'Winston Churchill has as much blood on his hands as the worst genocidal dictators, claims Indian politician' (referring to Dr Shashi Tharoor, author of 'Inglorious Empire'), Independent, 8 September 2017.
6. Andy Gregory, 'Britain misses its empire more than other post-colonial powers, new polling suggests', Independent, 11 March 2020.
7. Michael Boyle, 'I am a fourth-generation British black man. Yet still I'm made to feel I don't belong', Guardian, 31 October 2021.
8. Nigel Farage, interview with American news outlet Newsmax, 11 March 2021.
9. David Olusoga, 'The Royals are just like most of our press - trapped in a fantasy version of our past', Guardian, 14 March 2021.
10. Emma Kelly, 'Laurence Fox claims Sikh soldier in Sam Mendes war epic 1917 is "forcing diversity" on viewers', Metro, 20 January 2021.
11. Labour MP Tan Dhesi, 'Laurence Fox must apologise for bigoted 1917 views - 83,000 Sikhs died for Britain', Daily Mirror, 23 January 2020.
12. Tim Adams, 'Doreen Lawrence: "I could have shut myself away, but that is not me"', interview with Doreen Lawrence, Guardian, 20 April 2013.
13. Diane Roberts, 'Revisiting history: the troubling side of the venerable country house', Prospect magazine, 4 October 2021.
14. Sathnam Sanghera, 'Empireland - how imperialism has shaped modern Britain', 2021, Viking Penguin, p.61.
15. Jonathan Owen, 'British Empire: Students should be taught colonialism "not all good", say historians', Independent, 22 January 2016.

CHAPTER EIGHT

1. Liz Thomas, 'Public school singers take over the pop charts: 60 per cent of acts are now privately educated', Mail Online, 5 December 2010.
2. Stuart Maconie, 'The Nanny State Made Me - A Story of Britain and How to Save It', Ebury Press, 2020, p.75.
3. Nick Duffell, 'Wounded leaders: British Elitism and the Entitlement Illusion - A psychohistory', Lone Arrow Press, 2014, Preface.
4. Robert Verkaik, 'Posh Boys: How English Public Schools Ruin Britain', Oneworld Publications, 2018, p.284.
5. Robert Verkaik, 'Posh Boys: How English Public Schools Ruin Britain', p.3.
6. Tony Parsons, 'Comprehensive Failure', GQ magazine, September 2010.
7. Frances Ryan, 'The real problem is that England's education system rewards the rich', Guardian, 18 August 2020.
8. 'Brown shoes and loud ties hinder investment banker hopefuls', BBC news website, 1 September 2016.
9. 'Less affluent kids are locked out of investment banking jobs', Social Mobility Commission press release, 1 September 2016.
10. 'Socio-Economic Diversity in Life Sciences and Investment Banking', Social Mobility Commission, July 2016.
11. 'Navigating the Labyrinth: socio-economic background and career progression within the Civil Service', Social Mobility Commission report, May 2021.

12. James Gale and James Gillespie, 'Private schools upstage the West End with cutting-edge theatres', Sunday Times, 10 September 2017.
13. Lucy Higginson, 'Luxury hotel or boarding school dorm?', Daily Telegraph, 22 September 2015.
14. Francis Green and David Kynaston, 'Engines of Privilege: Britain's Private School Problem', Bloomsbury, 2019, p.93.
15. Francis Green and David Kynaston, 'Engines of Privilege: Britain's Private School Problem', p.100.
16. Fiona Miller, 'Eton, we have a problem', New European, 17 March 2022.
17. 'Expensive Education: what are the most expensive private schools in the country, and is it more expensive for boys or girls?' PoundToy survey, 6 April 2021.
18. Robert Watts and Sian Griffiths, 'Private School Pay List: rise of £100,000 salaries sparks fears of brain drain', Sunday Times, 7 March 2021.
19. Dr Aaron Reeves and Dr Sam Friedman,'The dogged persistence of the British "old boy": how private school alumni reach the elite', (referenced in the Conversation), London School of Economics study, 31 October 2017.
20. Haroon Siddique, 'Who's Who study sheds new light on power of old boy network', Guardian, 30 October 2017.
21. Robert Verkaik, 'Posh Boys: How English Public Schools Ruin Britain', p.23.
22. Robert Verkaik, 'Posh Boys: How British Public Schools Ruin Britain', p.30.
23. Andrew Adonis, former Education Minister, 'Whole cities and towns are in grip of a social crisis', Yorkshire Post, 28 February 2019.
24. Michael Gove, 'Put VAT on school fees and soak the rich', Times, 24 February 2017.
25. Kiran Samrai, 'One 16-year-old isn't the problem with private education: Britain's system of inequality is', Prospect magazine, 23 January 2019.
26. Gavin O.,'Scholarships do remarkably little to make private schools more socially inclusive, study finds', FE News, 13 April 2021.
27. Sascha Lavin and Ian Overton, 'Elite private schools increase assets by more than half a billion pounds in six years', Byline Times, 25 November 2021.
28. Joris Luyendijk, 'How I learnt to loathe England: a Dutchman reflects on what he's learnt by living in England for six years - it isn't pretty', Prospect magazine, 6 October 2017.
29. Mehdi Hassan, 'Warren Buffet is Right: it's Time to Ban Private Schools', Huff Post ('the Blog'), 6 September 2012.
30. Alison Flood, 'Alan Bennett launches fierce attack on private education', Guardian, 17 June 2014.
31. Michael Gove, 'Put VAT on school fees and soak the rich', Times, 24 February 2017.
32. Stuart Maconie, 'The Nanny State Made Me - A Story of Britain and How to Save It', Ebury Press, 2020, p.74.
33. The Newsom Report (1968), the Public Schools Commission, First Report, Her Majesty's Stationary Office 1968.
34. Matthew Parris, 'Schools that sell privilege can't be charities', Times, 9 June 2012.
35. The Newsom Report (1968), the Public Schools Commission, First Report, Her Majesty's Stationary Office 1968.
36. Francis Green and David Kynaston, 'Engines of Privilege: Britain's Private School Problem', Bloomsbury, 2019, pp.173-174.
37. Lee Elliot Major and Stephen Machin, 'Only radical reform can fix Britain's broken ladder of social mobility', Guardian, 7 October 2020.
38. Tony Parsons, 'Comprehensive Failure', GQ magazine, September 2010.
39. Alan Rusbridger, 'Oxford University must become more diverse. But we're on the right path', Guardian, 21 May 2019.

40. Lee Elliot Major and Stephen Machin, 'What do we know and what should we do about Social Mobility?' Sage Publications Ltd, 2020, pp.85-86.

CHAPTER NINE

1. Andria Zafirakou, 'Those Who Can, Teach: What it Takes to Make the Next Generation', Bloomsbury Publishing, 2021, p.90.
2. 'Global Teacher Status Index 2018', The Varkey Foundation.
3. Camilla Turner, 'Highest graduate starting salary hits £60,000 for the first time', the Daily Telegraph, 21 January 2019.
4. 'English schools are struggling to retain newly qualified teachers', Economist, 9 August 2018.
5. Laura McInerney, 'Golden handcuffs for teachers won't solve the staffing crisis in our schools', Guardian, 28 February 2016.
6. Simon Hepburn, 'Recruiting Teachers', independently published, April 2020.
7. 'More teachers reporting mental health problems than ever', UCL News, 28 January 2020.
8. From the same source.
9. Francis Gilbert, 'Here's the real reason why teachers are quitting (it's not just the money)', the Conversation, 1 March 2016.
10. Kate Clanchy, 'Some Kids I Taught and What they Taught Me', Swift Press, 2022.
11. Jumbo Chan, 'Solving the teaching crisis has to start by treating us like professionals,' New Statesman, 22 March 2017.
12. Richard Adams, 'Repair bill for schools in England doubles to over £11 billion finds survey', Guardian, 27 May 2021.
13. Lynsey Hanley, 'Respectable', Penguin Books, 2016, p.88.
14. 'School' documentary on BBC 2, Series 1, Episode 3, first broadcast on 16 November 2018.
15. Patrick Butler, 'No grammar schools, lots of play: the secrets of Europe's top education system', Guardian, 20 September 2016.
16. 'Finland: a non-competitive education for a competitive economy' OECD 2014, p.175.
17. Dame Alison Peacock DL, DLitt, Chief Executive at Chartered College of Teaching, 'Support teachers - now is not the time for criticism', posted on LinkedIn, 1 May 2020.
18. Professor Peter Dolton, University of Sussex, Dr Robert De Vries, University of Kent, 'Reading between the lines - what the world really thinks of teachers', Varkey Foundation, 2020.

CHAPTER TEN

1. Daniel Susskind, 'A World Without Work - Technology, Automation and How We Should Respond', Allen Lane, 2020, p.1.
2. Daniel Susskind, 'A World Without Work - Technology, Automation and How We Should Respond', p.2.
3. Rupert Neate, 'Do smart supermarkets herald the end of shopping as we know it?' Guardian, 9 January 2022.
4. Aaron Morby, 'Balfour predicts largely worker-free sites by 2050', Construction Enquirer, 27 June 2017.
5. Louis Wustemann, 'A licence to print houses: 3D printing is being used to build homes faster and more cheaply than is possible with traditional methods', Financial Times, 30 December 2021.
6. Sarah Chambers, 'Harper Adams/Precision Decisions researchers prove it's possible to grow a crop without setting foot in field as Hands Free Hectare is harvested', Eastern Daily Press, 11 September 2017.

7. Daniel Susskind, 'A World Without Work - Technology, Automation and How We Should Respond', p.5.
8. Clive Cookson and Oli Elliott, 'Can Boris Johnson turn Britain into a technology leader?' Financial Times, 28 September 2021.
9. Creative UK: statistics https://www.jrf.org.uk/data/overall-uk-poverty-rates.
10. Hasan Bakhshi, Carl Benedikt Frey and Michael Osborne, Nesta Study: Creativity vs Robots - the Creative Economy and the Future of Employment, April 2015. https://media.nesta.org.uk/documents/creativity_vs._robots_wv.pdf.
11. BBC Arts website: Get Creative 'Take the Feel Good Test to improve your wellbeing' 8 May 2019. https://www.bbc.co.uk/programmes/articles/h0Wf2JL3GnG52jLp7j1ydk/take-the-feel-good-test-to-improve-your-wellbeing.
12. Cultural Learning Alliance website, 13 August 2021: 'Arts GCSE and A Level entries 2021' https://www.culturallearningalliance.org.uk/arts-gcse-and-a-level-entries-2021.
13. Cultural Learning Alliance Briefing Paper No.4, 'The Arts in Schools - why the arts matter in our education system' 2018. https://www.culturallearningalliance.org.uk/briefings.
14. 'You Won't Believe What Obama Says In This Video!'. BuzzFeedVideo on YouTube: https://www.youtube.com/watch?v=cQ54GDm1eL0.
15. Nina Schick, 'Deep Fakes and Infocalypse - What You Urgently Need to Know', Monoray, 2020, p.10.
16. Ruby Lott-Lavigna, 'BBC Says It Would Interview Flat-Earthers to be Impartial', Vice News, 12 January 2022.
17. Jon Henley, 'How Finland starts its fight against fake news in primary schools', Guardian, 29 January 2020.
18. Media Literacy Index 2021, Open Society Institute, Sofia https://osis.bg/?p=3750&lang=en.
19. Emma Charlton, 'How Finland is fighting fake news - in the classroom', The European Sting in collaboration with the World Economic Forum, 21 May 2019.
20. Richard Garner, 'Political education classes 'should be compulsory', Independent, 23 April 2011.
21. Dr James Weinberg, 'The Missing Link: an updated of the provision, practice and politics of democratic education in English secondary schools', University of Sheffield, November 2021. Commissioned by Shout Out UK, the University of Sheffield, Speaking Citizens and the University of Sussex.
22. House of Lords Select Committee on Citizenship and Civic Engagement, Report of Session 2017-19, 'The Ties that Bind: Citizenship and Civic Engagement in the 21st Century', 18 April 2018. House of Lords - The Ties that Bind: Citizenship and Civic Engagement in the 21st Century - Select Committee on Citizenship and Civic Engagement (parliament.uk)
23. From the same source.
24. David Wallace-Wells, 'The Uninhabitable Earth: A Story of the Future', Allen Lane, 2019, p.28.
25. Tom Wall, 'This is a wake-up call': the villagers who could be Britain's first climate refugees', Guardian, 18 May 2019.
26. Tessa Richards, 'Climate change could flood London any time after 2030 warns expert', British Medical Journal, 24 May 2008.
27. Robin McKie, 'Nearly half of Britain's biodiversity has gone since Industrial Revolution, Guardian, 10 October 2021.
28. Prof. Andrew Charlton-Perez, 'The Climate-change gaps in the UK school curriculum', guest post in the Carbon Brief, 15 September 2021, www.carbonbrief.org.
29. Meryl Batchelder, 'If children are to live with the climate crisis we must green the curriculum', the Guardian, 19 August 2021.

30. 'Teaching the Future - Research with UK teachers on the current state and future of climate education' February 2021, https://www.teachthefuture.uk/research.
31. Fiona Harvey, 'UK pupils failed by schools' teaching of climate crisis, experts say', the Guardian, 28 January 2022.

CONCLUSION

1. Joseph Rowntree Foundation website https://www.jrf.org.uk/data/overall-uk-poverty-rates.
2. Michael Marmot, 'Studying health inequalities has been my life's work. What's about to happen in the UK is unprecedented', Guardian, 8 April 2022.
3. 'New global ranking for life expectancy shows decades-long UK decline', Journal of the Royal Society of Medicine, 16 March 2023.
4. John Burn-Murdoch, 'Britons have the worst access to medical care in Europe', Financial Times, 4 November 2022.
5. Jonty Bloom, 'The UK's industrial disease', New European, 21 April 2022.
6. 'The shrinkflation state: the British state will soon cost more, yet provide less', Bagehot column, Economist, 19 February 2022.
7. Dave Harvey, 'Honda workers in Swindon to face "reality check" after it closes', BBC News website, 28 July 2021.
8. 'Why the UK must associate to Horizon Europe', policy paper, the Royal Society, December 2019.
9. Nick Pearce, 'The past is another country: busting the myth of Global Britain', New Statesman, 9 April 2018.
10. Simon Kuper, 'Why the English are complacent and the French are apocalyptic - England's postwar descent down the global hierarchy generated not apocalyptic thinking but declinism', Financial Times, 13 May 2021.
11. Joris Luyendijk, 'England, you lot need a good occupation: the country plainly needs to change. So hear me out on a gloriously revolutionary suggestion', Prospect magazine, 19 January 2017.
12. Andrew Kersley, 'Working class representation in UK journalism hits record low, report says', Press Gazette, 5 May 2022.
13. Fiona Hill, 'There is Nothing For You Here: Finding Opportunity in the Twentieth-First Century', Mariner Books, 2021, p.17.
14. Joris Luyendijk, 'How I learnt to loathe England: A Dutchman reflects on what he's learnt from living in Britain for the past six years - it isn't pretty', Prospect magazine, 6 October 2017.
15. Fiona Hill, 'There is Nothing For You Here: Finding Opportunity in the Twentieth-First Century', Mariner Books, 2021, p.13.
16. Professor Thomas Otte, 'The UK's international future', University of East Anglia, 2 February 2017. YouTube video description: 'Professor Thomas Otte, UEA, imagines the UK's international future through the eyes of a UK diplomat, famous for his clear-sighted vision'

Printed in Poland
by Amazon Fulfillment
Poland Sp. z o.o., Wrocław

24359802R00161